MORE
RAB C. NESBITT
SCRIPTS

MORE
Rab C. Nesbitt
SCRIPTS

IAN PATTISON

BBC BOOKS

Thanks, once again, to Colin Gilbert for producing and directing
Rab C. Nesbitt Series 2 on television and to Marcus Way for
taking the photographs.

Ian Pattison, March 1992

Published by BBC Books,
a division of BBC Enterprises Limited,
Woodlands, 80 Wood Lane, London W12 0TT
First published 1992

Designed by Hammond Hammond

Cover and inside photographs by Marcus Way

ISBN 0 563 36479 3

Set in 10/11 Sabon by Redwood Press Limited,
Melksham, Wiltshire. Printed and bound by
Redwood Press Limited, Melksham, Wiltshire.
Cover printed by Clays Limited, St Ives plc

CONTENTS

EPISODE ONE
Ethics

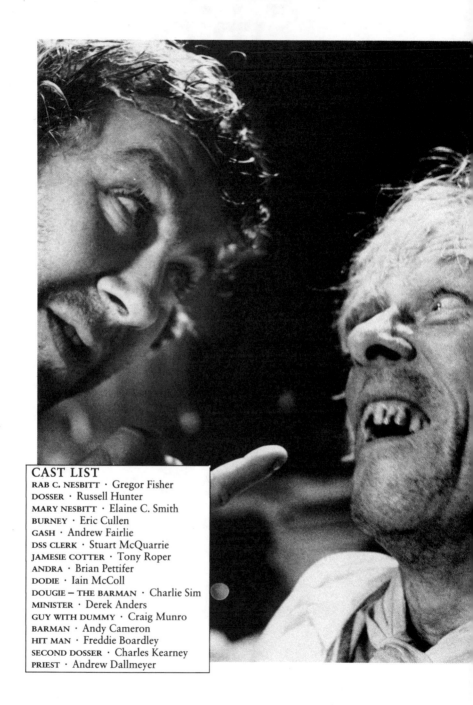

CAST LIST

RAB C. NESBITT · Gregor Fisher
DOSSER · Russell Hunter
MARY NESBITT · Elaine C. Smith
BURNEY · Eric Cullen
GASH · Andrew Fairlie
DSS CLERK · Stuart McQuarrie
JAMESIE COTTER · Tony Roper
ANDRA · Brian Pettifer
DODIE · Iain McColl
DOUGIE – THE BARMAN · Charlie Sim
MINISTER · Derek Anders
GUY WITH DUMMY · Craig Munro
BARMAN · Andy Cameron
HIT MAN · Freddie Boardley
SECOND DOSSER · Charles Kearney
PRIEST · Andrew Dallmeyer

SCENE 1. Govan street. Day.

The ugly side of Govan. We see dogs raking through middens. Alcoholics (real ones) are gathered on the corner waiting for the off-licence to open. Garbage in the street. Boarded up windows, weeds and rubbish strewn.

Music over the street noises. 'Morning', by Grieg, builds to its crescendo.

SCENE 2. A Govan street doorway. Day.

Music. 'Morning' is still playing.

An extremely messy, rubbish-strewn doorway.

Out of the garbage as the music swells rises Nesbitt. He stretches, opens out and blossoms slowly.

He looks about him, satisfied.

We get a pan of the street.

NESBITT. (*Stepping out of the garbage.*)Tell yi wan thing. See Sunday mornings like these, they make yi feel glad to be half alive! Honest to God, it's wan of thae days where yi only see the positive things in life, know what I mean? Thur a bright golden haze on the meadow. And Maggie Thatcher's 'effed off. And yi can see the improvement in Govan already, can't yi? (*He picks up a discarded newspaper.*) I mean, look at this. (*Points to headline.*) John Major says, 'I aim to make Britain a classless society.' Well he's made a bliddy good start in Govan. We've no class at all!

(*Moves off, singing.*) Zipedee do dah...!

SCENE 3. Riverside. Day.

Moments later. Nesbitt walking by the river edge.

NESBITT. (*To audience.*) Some place the Govan eh? There's no place like home! Which is perfectly correct as it happens coz I was born and brought up here and it's no place like home as I remember it. But then that's the nineties. The outer landscape changes and so does the inner one. I mean, fur roon my liver, two ulcers and a brain scan, I'm not exactly the rock of ages myself, am I?

A dosser shuffles out, cross: , Nesbitt's path, just ahead of him.

(*To audience.*) Some things yi can always rely on though. (*Indicating to dosser.*) The Sunday morning slop brain doing the south side shuffle there. (*Calls to dosser.*) Awright pal?

DOSSER. Eh?

NESBITT. (*Proffering coin.*) No worries, my man. I know how yi feel. Get any more dehydrated and yi could use yir balls for trail mix.

(*Still proffering coin.*) Look, here a wee bung. You wet your neck.

DOSSER. (*Looks at coin*) I don't want your charity. Did I ask you for a handout? That's the whole trouble with this society. All it knows how to give you is money!

NESBITT. That a fact? Canny say I've had much trouble in that direction myself.

DOSSER. Well it's too late for money now.

He knocks the coin from Nesbitt's hand.

DOSSER. See you in hell!

The dosser leaps into the river.

NESBITT. (*Looking into river.*) Yi awright?

We see bubbles rising from the water. There is no sign of the dosser.

(*To audience*) Stupid what yi shout in these situations, in't it? (*Looks into river*) Haw! Ya selfish swine that yi are! Don't droon! If yi droon I'm gonny feel dead guilty! (*To audience.*) Ach, bugger it!

Nesbitt plunges into the water.

SCENE 4. Riverside. Day.

The riverside. Nesbitt is administering chest massage to the dosser. Frantic, he abandons the traditional 'hands on' method and administers a 'nut to the belly' technique.

NESBITT. (*Desperate.*) C'mon, ya mockit bam! Wake up! The very least yi can do is speak to me! Say something!

The Dosser opens his eyes and sprays a jet of water into Nesbitt's face.

DOSSER. Bastard!

NESBITT. Eh? What'd yi mean? What'd yi mean?

DOSSER. I mean it's taken me years to find the courage to do what I just did. I'll never be able to find the nerve again!

NESBITT. Ya ungrateful bam! I just saved your poxy life!

DOSSER. Exactly. Saved it for what? Eh?

(Nesbitt is at a loss.)

DOSSER. I didn't want my life. But you're the one that saved it. So from this moment on it's your responsibility. Where you go, I go. Where you sleep, I sleep. What do you think about that? Go on, say something! *(Mimicking Nesbitt.)* The very least you can do is speak to me!

NESBITT. *(Explodes.)* Bastard!

DOSSER. Correction. *Homeless* bastard. *(Rubbing his hands.)* Now, where do we eat?

SCENE 5. The Nesbitts' living room.

The dosser is at the table wolfing food greedily. The family (Gash, Burney, Mary) are watching him in horrified fascination.

MARY. *(Politely, to dosser.)* Yi enjoying that?

BURNEY. Enjoying it? He couldnie make more noise if he sooked it up using his arse for a hoover.

MARY. Shuttit you! That man's homeless!

GASH. His fleas urnie. *(Picking one out.)* They're using my soup as a swimming pool.

Mary shudders. She drags Nesbitt by the lapel to one side.

MARY. *(To Nesbitt.)* C'mere you, I want to speak to you.

NESBITT. What is it? What's the matter?

MARY. What's the matter? Just who is this gink and what's he

I know you're honest and above board but I'm still not voting conservative, Mr. Patten.

doing with his rancid feet under oor table?

NESBITT. I telt yi, Mary, he's a wee mate. I just happened to bump into him in the middle of . . .

MARY. The Clyde? I know! What the hell were yi doing in there?

NESBITT. Water-skiing on a pizza lid! What the hell'd yi think I was doing, I fell in, din't I?

MARY. Well I don't know what's going on here. But if yi ask me, you've fell in a helluva lot deeper than yi bargained for. Coz see that (*Indicating to dosser.*), I widnae trust that as far as I could fling you.

NESBITT. Ach, don't be like that Mary. He's just a poor old sowel that's doon on his luck, that's all. (*To dosser, waving.*) In't that right, compadre!

DOSSER. Don't you worry aboot me, Rab. I'm just entertaining the weans here!

The dosser picks fleas from his hair and flicks them at Gash and Burney.

GASH & BURNEY. Aya! Get tae...!

NESBITT. Let him stay, Mary. Just for a wee tate. Yi know what they say. There but for the grace of the big fella...

MARY. (*To Nesbitt.*) Awright well. But just for a wee tate. I mean it! (*She goes.*)

NESBITT. At's the gemme, Mary hen. Yi'll hardly know he's here!

The dosser appears, and comes up really close to Nesbitt. Nesbitt's face registers the stink.

DOSSER. How goes it, Rab? What's the verdict?

NESBITT. Great news, my man! Yi can stay the night.

DOSSER. The night? Oh no, I don't think so Rab.

NESBITT. Whit'd yi mean, whit'd yi mean?

DOSSER. Well a puppy isn't only for Christmas, is it DADDY?

He growls at Nesbitt, who gives a little startled jump. The dosser nuzzles up, dog like, to Nesbitt.

Nesbitt ruffs his hair, tentatively. Looking uneasily to Mary, Gash and Burney who are watching.

NESBITT. (*Still ruffing his hair.*) There there ... there there ... son. (*To audience.*) Bastard!

SCENE 6. The DSS Office. Day.
A clerk is at the desk. Nesbitt stands opposite him. The dosser is sitting some way behind him.

NESBITT. (*To audience.*) Whit did you call me?

CLERK. Unreasonable. You're being unreasonable, Mr Nesbitt.

NESBITT. (*Slamming fist on desk.*) Yir arse! Now listen you to me. Don't you get above yirself. Yi know what they say – servility costs nothing!

CLERK. I'm sorry, Mr Nesbitt but rules are rules. And we've been forced to reduce your entitlement. To accommodate your change in circumstances.

NESBITT. What circumstances? I've never had circumstances in my life! Who the hell telt you I'd circumstances?

CLERK. Most of our tip-offs are anonymous, Mr Nesbitt. I'm afraid we don't live in a very ethical society.

NESBITT. Bliddy right we don't. And it's not a very fair one neither! I mean d'yi see that? (*He indicates to the dosser. Who waves back.*) I howked that lump of subhuman keech oot the gutter and pamped a roof ower its head! I splattered it with the milk of human kindness! Where was yir bliddy society then boy?

CLERK. I'm sorry Mr Nesbitt. If you want to take a lodger into your home that's your affair. But you must expect to pay the price.

NESBITT. (*Exploding*) But, he's not a lodger! Lodgers are big handsome bastards in tight jeans that drive trucks and try to slip yir wumman a length when your back's turned. I mean look at him. The last jump he had was in shock therapy!

DOSSER. (*Calling over.*) Are you talking aboot me. Don't you talk aboot me or I'm warning yi, I'll commit suicide!

NESBITT. (*To dosser. Calls back.*) Well yi better get a bliddy move on! Coz I might commit murder first! (*To clerk.*) D'yi see what I'm up against here? Do yi see what I'm up against? (*Nesbitt grabs clerk by the throat.*) Now we can do this the hard way, or else we can do it the psychotically deranged way! What's it gonny be?

CLERK. (*Fighting him off.*) You're wasting your time! Your threats fall on deaf ears!

He presses a button on the desk. An alarm bell clangs, loudly.

CLERK. Now if you're wise, you'll be gone before the police arrive!

NESBITT. Awright, I'm gawn, I'm gawn! Yi can stick yir money! Compassion is it? Humanity is it? I'll tell you this boy, youse people don't know the meaning of the word! But us scum do boy. Come roon oor hoose, you'll never go withoot a cup of tea. Fair enough, yi'll maybes have an impetigo scab as a biscuit, but it's the thought that counts, it's the thought! Coz scum's warm, boy! We ooze! (*Holding one hand out.*) We're aye ready with the open hand of friendship!

Good news for the homeless.

DOSSER. (*Standing by Nesbitt.*) That's the gemme, Rab. You tell him.

NESBITT. (*Makes a fist with the hand, speaks with great restraint to dosser.*) Shuttit you! And get up that bliddy road! (*To audience.*) It's just as well I've got an understanding wife.

SCENE 7. The Nesbitts' living room. Day.
Nesbitt and Mary are laying the table. Mary stops to study a letter.

MARY. They did what?

NESBITT. They ... cut wur benefit. (*Pointing to the letter.*) Says just there, look.

MARY. In the name ...!

NESBITT. I mean I widnae worry doll. We were getting too much money anyway. (*Noticing biscuits on the table.*) Look at that. I mean Jaffa cakes on a Wednesday, Mary. (*He picks up the packet.*) Pure decadence.

MARY. I had to lash oot on them, din't I? To make it up to the wean!

NESBITT. Make what up to the wean?

BURNEY. (*Appears from under the table.*) This, ya big swine!

He points to his head. He's bald, totally, and is wearing a headband.

NESBITT. Burney son! What's happened to yir hair?

BURNEY. Oh that? I sent it doon the shops for a jar of Brylcreem. Whit the hell di yi think happened to it? I'd to get it shaved aff. That old swine gied me ringworm, look!

He displays the back of his head. It has gentian violet on it.

NESBITT. (*Stubbornly.*) Garbage! I don't believe it!

MARY. It's true, Rab.

Gash enters. Nesbitt spies him. He seizes the opportunity to defend himself.

NESBITT. Yi see, there's Gash! There's nothing the matter with him is there? He husnie caught nothing!

GASH. Haw, Maw. Seen my crab ointment and my velvet Y-fronts?

He scratches his groin.

MARY. I mean it, Rab. He's got to go!

NESBITT. How?

MARY. That's your problem!

SCENE 8. Two Ways pub. Day.
Jamesie, Andra, Dodie, Nesbitt, at the bar. Dougie is behind the bar, serving.

The dosser sits at a table.

Nesbitt is looking troubled.

JAMESIE. Awright, Two Ways Mental Mensa, froth off lips.

Andra and Dodie wipe froth from their lips in unison, with a swift single finger movement.

JAMESIE. Next practice question. 'Where are the Seychelles?'

DODIE. On the say – shore! Sorry, boss, wee bit of light relief, know?

JAMESIE. Youse know the rules – nae relief afore a game! I'll gie yeez all the relief yeez want when yeez've lifted that coveted 'Danny's Chicken Bar Brain of Wine Alley Trophy'. Eh?

ANDRA & DODIE. Hull-oo!

JAMESIE. That's my boys! (*To Nesbitt.*) Yi could be doing with some relief yirself, Rab, judging by the length of yir fizzer. What's the matter?

NESBITT. Och, it's thon wee bit of business I telt yi aboot the other day. (*Noticing dosser.*) He's waving, look, say hullo.

JAMESIE. Oh that bloodsucking swine. (*Grinning warmly, waving back.*) Well I telt yi what to do aboot that, din't I?

NESBITT. What was that?

JAMESIE. (*Waving to dosser, calls.*) Awright faither, lovely to see yi again! (*To Nesbitt, matter of factly, in same breath.*) Kill him.

Govan is yours to discover. What are you waiting for, an invitation from the president?

NESBITT. What?

The dosser and Jamesie engage in a little visual mime banter as Jamesie speaks to Nesbitt.

JAMESIE. (*Bantering.*) Kill him. Top him. Chib him. Gie him the malky.

NESBITT. Away and don't talk stupid, I canny do that!

JAMESIE. Yi widnae have to. I've colleagues that'll do it for yi. Take it from me, Rab. This guy's gonny bleed yi dry. And let's face it, what's a dosser more or less in the world!

NESBITT. No Jamesie. No way. I'd sooner try diplomacy.

The dosser appears by Nesbitt.

DOSSER. Hey Rab, gie's three poun for a carry oot.

NESBITT. Three poun! I huvnie got...

DOSSER. (*Holding glass to his own wrist.*) Gie me it, or I'll not be responsible!

Nesbitt coughs up.

JAMESIE. (*Up close to Nesbitt.*) You try diplomacy, Rab. Then when that's failed come and see me aboot the malky.

Nesbitt bites his lip.

SCENE 9. Church. Day.
Minutes later. In the minister's study. The minister and Nesbitt are about to sit on opposite sides of a small desk. Religious artefacts prominent on the walls. Nesbitt is sorely troubled.

NESBITT. (*Sitting.*) Thanks very much for serving iz at short notice.

MINISTER. Not at all, Mr Nesbitt. Now what can I do for you?

NESBITT. I'll get right to the point, boss. I know you'll be busy ... taking in deliveries, or whatever it is youse people do through the week, know?

MINISTER. The point, Mr. Nesbitt.

NESBITT. Aye, well the fact is, I've got this wee problemette. It's driving me up the pole. I mean it'll be a piece of piss for a skilled moral tradesman like yourself, yi understand, but yea verily it's got my erse hinging oot the windae, I kid you not!

MINISTER. Calm yourself, Mr Nesbitt. (*Proffering plate.*) Here, have a Jaffa cake.

NESBITT. (*Demurring*) Naw thanks, yir awright. Look, to put it in a nutshell, I howked this homeless hughie oot the watter after he tried to take a heider aff the pierheid. Noo he's dipping my pocket with wan hon and pressing my guilt buttons with the other, and the upshot is it's caving in my napper, do I make myself clear?

MINISTER. You mean you're on the horns of a moral dilemma?

NESBITT. Got it in wan pal! I like your style. I'm gonny tell my mates aboot you, we've got hunners of moral dilemmas, I'll punt the business your way! You'll be opening up yir ain faith in no time! Right, what's the answer!

MINISTER. The answer? I'm afraid it's not that simple.

NESBITT. Whit'd yi mean? Whit'd yi mean? This is a church, in't it? If I'm thirsting after a swally I go to the pub, if I'm thirsting after righteousness I go to a church! I mean I'll pay, you know. I'm not on legal aid.

MINISTER. It's not a question of payment, Mr Nesbitt. It's a question of doing the right thing. The truth operates in shades of grey.

NESBITT. (*Whisking out an envelope.*) See that? That's my electric bill. That operates in shades of red, get my drift? Now for the last time. I've a homeless punter shacked up in my billet. If I put him oot, he tops himself, if I keep him, my weans go hungry. Now what am I gonny do?

MINISTER. Well let's see. On the one hand we've ... and on the other ... I've got it! Have you tried the Citizen's Advice Bureau?

NESBITT. (*Getting up.*) Skip it.

MINISTER. Look, Mr Nesbitt. I'm sorry we don't know all the answers. Most of us don't even know all the questions. But we're doing our best, believe me!

NESBITT. That a fact? Well when you've got a dosser kipping in your vestry, then we'll talk as equals. Until then, gie's peace! (*To audience.*) See that? It's thanks to the likes of that, that thousands of weans every Sunday are still falling asleep in bible class.

(*Calling back.*) Have a nice stupor!

Nesbitt slams the door shut. The vibration causes a large crucifix to drop off the wall. The minister gives a slight jump.

SCENE 10. The Nesbitts' living room. Night.
The Nesbitts' living room, in darkness. Nesbitt stands at the window, smoking. It's a very stormy night.

NESBITT. (*To audience.*) A wee long night of the soul, know? To be or not to be, that is the question. May-be or may-be not, that is the answer. I mind the time when life was simple. A song, a smile, a kicking in the lavvies. And I know yiv got to move with the times. But the malky! To do the malky. (*Holding up a knife.*) Is this a Stanley knife I see before me?

The dosser speaks. Startling him.

DOSSER. That you talking to yirself, Rab? That's a bad sign.

NESBITT. Look. I'm gonny put a proposition to you. And I'm gonny put it as considerately and as delicately as I know how.

DOSSER. What's the proposition?

NESBITT. Either bugger aff or else I'll gie yi the malky!

DOSSER. You? Do iz a favour. There's more wind and pish in you than's blowing doon that road oot there. Sleep well.

The dosser returns to bed.

NESBITT. (*To audience.*) Fair put the fear of God up him there, din't I?

SCENE 11. On the way to the pub. Day.
Nesbitt and Jamesie walking along the street. Dodie and Andra following behind.

JAMESIE. You sure you want to go through with this Rab?

NESBITT. Sure I'm sure. I've got no choice have I! This is the place?

JAMESIE. This is it Rab. Yi canny sling a rivet in there withoot

Rehearsing a few tragic expressions, prior to aproaching the DSS for a Crisis Loan.

hitting a man. When the yards shut doon it was either that or driving taxis. Trust me Rab, I know these people. Yi'll be awright as long as yi do as I do.

DODIE. Better start shitting yirself then, Rab.

JAMESIE. Look, away youse hame and rest yir brains for the night! This is the big boys' playground. Yir liable to get hurtit. (*To Nesbitt.*) 'Mon Rab, in we go.

Nesbitt goes to enter the pub.

No, not like that. Walk hard.

They walk hard to the door.

SCENE 12. Pub. Day.
The pub is busy. Very atmospheric, distinctive. It isn't the 'Two Ways'.

An ancient man in a wig with blood streaming down his face is singing...

Men are selling goods from suitcases. (Socks, radios, stereo systems, computers, etc.)

Man with a trendily dressed tailor's dummy is trying to interest a potential customer...

GUY WITH DUMMY. Honest pal. It's not nicked. It's an unwanted gift.

Nesbitt and Jamesie approach the bar. Jamesie speaks confidentially to the barman.

JAMESIE. I'm looking for somebody to do a murder, pal. Thur eighteen pence in it fur yi.

BARMAN. And I'm looking for somebody to buy a drink. Or thur a sore face in it for you.

NESBITT. (*Proffering cash.*) Two heavy.

BARMAN. That's the gemme.

Barman picks up hand microphone, speaks, matter of factly, to bar at large.

BARMAN. (*Through microphone.*) Block here looking for a murder, gents.

JAMESIE. Quiet!

BARMAN. (*Through microphone.*) Block here looking for a quiet murder, gents. Come on, come on! (*To Jamesie.*) Is it local?

Jamesie nods.

BARMAN. (*To Jamesie.*) That's good, nae boundary charge. (*To bar at large.*) Murder for Govan, gents. And can whoever takes it bring back a pint of milk from the all-night garage? Murder for Govan!

A hit man has drifted up to the bar. He wears a shell suit with a collar and tie underneath. Highlights, ear ring.

HIT MAN. Youse the clients?

JAMESIE. (*Nods.*) You the ... operative?

HIT MAN. (*Proffering card.*) Company card.

NESBITT. (*Peering at card. To Jamesie.*) What they called?

JAMESIE. Stiff-U-Like.

Nesbitt and Jamesie share a look. The hit man starts his sales pitch.

HIT MAN. Yi see, my man, what I offer is a complete service of the malky. I am no cowboy. Me, myself, personally, I have done many murders. I offer a full tariff according to choice. Stabbing, shooting or encased in concrete in the fly-over. Only with the concrete the price goes up coz of the fixed overheads. That's a wee joke, by the way, to relax the tension!

A squelching noise. The hit man sniffs.

What's that smell?

JAMESIE. (*Quietly.*) Nothing.

NESBITT. (*Gulps.*) When can yi do it?

SCENE 13. Two Ways pub. Evening.
We are shown a sign: 'TWO WAYS QUIZ NIGHT'.

For the last time, I don't give a toss what happened to your pension fund — I am *not* Robert Maxwell!

In the bar an air of expectancy hangs among the clientele. Three ugly old cheerleaders are chanting: 'Two Ways, Two Ways, thur's no Two Ways aboot it'.

We then see Jamesie, Andra and Dodie, in track-suits, limbering up like footballers.

A man gives some money to Jamesie.

Dougie the barman spots this from behind the bar.

JAMESIE. (*To man.*) Cheers, pal. No worries.

DOUGIE. Here Cotter! I hope you're not running a book on this. I'm not licensed for gambling!

JAMESIE. That is a slur, Dougie. This dosh is for the sick weans! So's we can buy them a university or some Rolos or something!

A 'boo' goes up.

ANDRA. Look. Here the opposition!

DODIE. Who we playing anyway, Jamesie. Yi never said?

JAMESIE. Ach, just some bunch of basket weaving old lags fresh oot of Barlinnie. Relax, we'll take them apart.

DOUGIE. (*To bar at large, through microphone.*) Will you welcome, with degrees in literature, political philosophy and nuclear physics, the ex-Barlinnie Special Unit All Stars!

A roar. The All Stars wave, sit down at a table.

JAMESIE. (*Gulps.*) Of course winning isnae everything. It's the taking part that coonts.

DOUGIE. (*Through microphone introducing.*) And your very own Two Ways Pure Mad Mental Mensa!

A roar goes up.

JAMESIE. Right boys, wire rims on.

Jamesie, Nesbitt, Andra and Dodie don wire rim specs.

... Now, let's get oot there and cogitate!

SCENE 14. Riverside. Night. Same place as SCENE 3.
Nesbitt sitting by the water's edge, on a capstan.

NESBITT. (*To audience.*) I expect yeez'd like to know what it feels like to get somebody bumped off. It disnae feel of anything, actually. I suspect it'll be like getting yir Nat King for the first time. Not up to much but yi think aboot nothing else for months afterwards.

The hit man appears.

HIT MAN. (*Motions to a distant figure standing by the water.*) That him?

NESBITT. Aye. How yi gonny do it?

HIT MAN. (*Showing a bat.*) I'm gonny hit him ower the heid with a baseball bat.

He goes.

NESBITT. (*To audience.*) The appliance of science, eh? (*He rises.*) Queer life awthegither, in't it? One minute yir gie'ing a guy ten pence to keep him alive, the next yir paying thirty quid to get him knocked off. D'yi think I might've taken a wrang turning somewhere?

Nesbitt takes a step, bumps into a second dosser who's standing by the water's edge.

Sorry, pal. Yi awright?

SECOND DOSSER. Eh?

NESBITT. (*Proffering coin.*) Look, here a wee bung. You wet yir neck.

SECOND DOSSER. (*Looks at coin.*) I don't want your charity. Did I ask you for a handout? That's the whole trouble with this society. All it knows how to give you is money! (*He prepares to take the plunge.*) See you in hell!

NESBITT. (*Grabbing him by the collar.*) Haw, haw, save yirsel a wetting. I've seen this picture.

SECOND DOSSER. Oh yi have? Ach well, win some lose some. There's usually some silly bastard that gets taken in and offers yi a bed for a while.

NESBITT. Oh is that a fact! Well this silly bastard's just paid thirty notes to get the other half of your double act the severe malky! (*Realisation dawns.*) Christ!

SCENE 15. Riverside. Night. Same time – a short distance away.

The dosser is on the ground with a gag around his mouth. The hit man pulls back the baseball bat to hit him.

A hand grabs it, preventing him.

NESBITT. (*For it is he.*) Listen pal. I hate to disturb a man at his work. But there's been a wee minor cock up. Could yi desist forthwith?

HIT MAN. Look, sur, I am a professional. When I start a job, I finish it.

NESBITT. Look, take the money! Forget the malky. It's been worth it just to see a craftsman at work.

HIT MAN. Look, I don't think you understand. I'm not in this game for the money. I like to uphold the amateur ideals. Casual homicide is my life. *You* keep the money. I'll do the malky!

NESBITT. I'd an awfie funny feeling you'd say that, know?

Nesbitt batters him on the head with a dustbin lid. We hear the appropriate sound effect.

NESBITT. (*To audience.*) My second clanger of the night, know?

(*To dosser.*) And you beat it pronto, or you'll get the same!

Both dossers scarper, pronto. Dosser one calls back.

DOSSER. No hard feelings, Rab. It was nothing personal!

NESBITT. Get tae . . . !

The hit man suddenly leaps into river.

Nesbitt peers over the parapet into the black waters and calls . . .

NESBITT. Haw pal! Yi awright?

The Chairman of Glasgow Council about to refute allegations that the city is populated by cultural stereotypes.

We hear the sound of bubbles.

(*To audience.*) And I always thought shite floated.

SCENE 16. Pub. Night.
The Two Ways pub as before. Quiz night is winding up. The scores are seen above the teams.

DOUGIE. (*Through microphone.*) And with the scores neck and neck at Barlinnie All Stars ... 99, Two Ways ... nil, we come to the Mensa's last three questions of the contest.

JAMESIE. Right boys, go for the burn!

DOUGIE. Who wrote *Oliver Twist*?

They look at each other, blankly.

Dougie tries another question.

DOUGIE. Where are the Cairngorms?

More blank looks.

DOUGIE. ... And finally, the last question of the contest. How do you claim a Crisis Loan at the DSS if you haven't filled in a B1 Form?

Their hands shoot up simultaneously, as they strain from their seats bursting with knowledge.

DOUGIE. Two Ways, Cotter.

JAMESIE. It's a trick question, yi canny!

DOUGIE. Correct. And at the end of the contest the All Stars have 99 and the Two Ways have, apart from egg all over their faces, two points!

JAMESIE. Never mind boys. It was a quality two. We go oot that door with wur heids held high!

The crowd boo. A glass whistles over their heads. They duck.

JAMESIE. Quick boys, oot the lavvy windae!

The Two Ways team sneak away as glass explodes against walls.

SCENE 17. Church confessional. Day.

Nesbitt is in a confessional booth. Religious music plays softly in the background.

NESBITT. (*To audience.*) See when yi get right down to it, yir conscience is like a Provident Line. Yir better to settle up pronto or the repayments get higher and higher, know what I mean?

A shutter is lifted.

... Bless me, Jim, for I have sinned.

PRIEST. (*Speaks out of the darkness, not yet visible.*) How have you sinned, my son?

NESBITT. I malkied a block called Spud McKechron. They fished his arse oot the watter with a boat hook this morning at Wemyss Bay.

PRIEST. Spud McKechron? That murdering bastard. He's been asking for it for years.

NESBITT. Eh?

PRIEST. In fact I'd be grateful if you'd go for the double.

NESBITT. Whit'd yi mean? Whit'd yi mean?

The priest pokes his head into the light for the first time.

We see he's the man at the quiz night who was giving money to Jamesie.

PRIEST. Get that bastard Jamesie Cotter. I bet a week's collection money he'd win at the Two Ways Quiz Night. (*Proffering money.*) Here's thirty quid. What'd you say?

Nesbitt looks at the priest, looks at the notes. He nuts the priest, takes the notes.

NESBITT. (*To audience.*) Ethics, eh? More bliddy trouble than they're worth. (*He tears up the money, throws it in the air.*) ... Pure again!

Country

CAST LIST

OLD MAN · John Young
OLD WOMAN · Jean Faulds
MARY NESBITT · Elaine C. Smith
JAMESIE COTTER · Tony Roper
DODIE · Iain McColl
ANDRA · Brian Pettifer
BURNEY · Eric Cullen
RAB C. NESBITT · Gregor Fisher
OLD PUNTER · Cliff Hanley
ASSISTANT · Forbes Masson
RUSTIC · Bruce Morton
ELLA COTTER · Barbara Rafferty
GASH · Andrew Fairlie
GIRL 1 · Victoria Nairn
GIRL 2 · Ashley Jensen
NICKY – THE HANDSOME BASTARD · Vincent Friell
LOCAL IN BAR/RED BEARD · Billy Riddoch
BARMAN · Lee Cornes
CLIMBER 1 · Trevor Neal
CLIMBER 2 · Simon Hickson
A BUSH/MILITARY MAN · Jonathan Kydd
CROFTER 1 · Jim Byars
BOY · Alexander Nelson

SCENE 1. Living room of old couple. Evening.

Two old punters are lying on their living room floor, stranded, banging with walking sticks. Loud voices can be heard from next door.

OLD MAN. Help! Help! (*To old woman.*) This is getting embarrassing. The fourth fall this week. The poor Mrs Nesbitt'll be getting sick of us.

OLD WOMAN. Aye, the poor sowel's worn out. She could do with getting away from it all.

OLD MAN. Aye. Look, why don't we give her a wee break? Give her the car and the keys to the cottage and let her take the family away for the weekend.

OLD WOMAN. The cottage? I don't know. Is the cottage still habitable?

OLD MAN. Of course it's habitable! I checked it only recently.

OLD WOMAN. How recently?

OLD MAN. Let's see. What year was Chernobyl?

They puzzle. The door bursts open. Mary bursts in looking harassed.

MARY. Oh, in the name! Have yeez been doon there long? Only I couldnie hear yi banging for that rammy next door in my hoose.

OLD MAN. Aye. What are they doing in there?

MARY. (*Helping him up.*) Don't ask.

SCENE 2. The Nesbitts' living room. Evening.
(*Meanwhile.*)

The television is on. It's showing American football. Jamesie, Dodie and Andra sit watching intently. Somebody gets a touch down.

JAMESIE. Yo!

DODIE. Wooooooo!

ANDRA. Woo! Woo! Woo! Woo!

They slap skin.

JAMESIE. Brilliant this in't it boys! American fitba!

ANDRA. Yi can get right mowed in and give it laldy!

DODIE. Brill! (*To Burney.*) Yi enjoying yirself son?

BURNEY. (*Unimpressed.*) Aye, brill. What's the score, by the way?

DODIE. The Redsox are in a two and one situation and they're looking for a pinch hit-off, a loaded base.

JAMESIE. Naw, naw, that's no right Dodie.

DODIE. How no? How no?

JAMESIE. That's baseball. That's the wrang sport. This is fitba.

DODIE. Oh right. Well what is the score well?

Jamesie and Dodie look to Andra.

ANDRA. Don't look at me. I just came here to whoop.

JAMESIE. Andra's right. Thur no point getting bogged doon with details, let's just enjoy wurselves. Yo! (*Lifting can.*) Yo!

DODIE. Wooooooooo!

ANDRA. Woo! Woo! Woo! Woo! (*To Burney.*) C'mon Burney son, let yirself go. Get into the spirit of things.

BURNEY. Fair enough.

(*Stomping feet. Face filled with hate, pointing finger at screen, chanting in football style.*)

Who's the bastard in the white! Who's the bastard in the white!

Disapproving looks from the others.

... Did I say something wrong?

SCENE 3. Fast food joint. Evening.
Nesbitt in queue. Two boys in front of him dressed in shell suits, baseball caps turned back to front.

NESBITT. (*To audience.*) Look at that, eh? Did yi ever see anything more irritating and pretentious than thon in all yir puff? Since

When I had nothing I believed in Scottish Socialism. And now that I'm a millionaire, I believe in it even more.

when did we suddenly become the fifty-fourth state of America, that's what I want to know. Tell yi one thing, I'm glad to come from a generation that stonds up for the old values, know what I mean?

We cut to the counter. A very old punter is being served. He wears a bonnet that's on back to front. A young trendy is serving him.

OLD PUNTER. (*Very fragile.*) And six cans of Budweiser.

ASSISTANT. (*Serving up cans very condescendingly.*) Superbowl?

OLD PUNTER. I widnae miss it!

ASSISTANT. (*Counting out change.*) There you go Mr McAllister, better get off home before they finish the time out. Have a nice day!

OLD PUNTER. (*At door.*) Right on!

ASSISTANT. (*To Nesbitt, chuckling indulgently.*) Seventy-three. Wonderful old character, eh? Marvellous spirit.

NESBITT. Yi think so? Irritating old bastard if yi ask me. Hope to Christ I don't end up like that.

Tut tuts from assistant.

... What are you tut tutting at, when I'm his age, Amazonia might be trendy and I'll be scudding in and oot of here in the buff with a blowpipe and a shrunken heid on my belt, and yi widnae fancy that, wid yi, NAW!

ASSISTANT. Let's face it, it wouldn't be the first time.

NESBITT. Don't give iz yir lip. It widnae be 'wonderful old character, marvellous spirit' then. Yi'd be howking that shotgun oot from under the coonter and blasting the woad aff my arse afore yi could say ethnic minority! I know your type!

ASSISTANT. I beg your pardon. I don't keep a shotgun under my counter.

NESBITT. Is that a fact? (*Producing a gun.*) Empty yir till well.

Frozen look from assistant. Nesbitt, laughing, squirts water into assistant's face.

NESBITT. Helluva sorry. See once yi get a hod of one of thae things, yi canny stop! (*To frosty faced woman in queue.*) I love a laugh. Yi like a laugh yirself hen? (*Considering her face.*) You widnae know. Bit ootside your experience eh?

ASSISTANT. (*To Nesbitt.*) Look, do you want something or don't you?

NESBITT. Certainly I want something! Of course I want something! I've got a list here from my pals, hin't I? (*Opens out list.*) Let's see, gies four bags of (*Reading it all wrong.*) Mignons morceaux.

ASSISTANT. What? (*Looks at list.*) Oh, mignons morceaux.

NESBITT. 'At's them. And three bags of tackys.

ASSISTANT. Tacos.

NESBITT. Aye. And whatever that says there, look.

ASSISTANT. (*Reading.*) A pakora.

NESBITT. A pakora? Yi sure? What the hell is a pakora by the way?

Can I not even have a fly ham shank in peace?

ASSISTANT. A pakora is a spicy vegetable package shaped like a meatball.

NESBITT. Is that a fact! God wait till I see that councillor.

ASSISTANT. How do you mean?

NESBITT. He telt me it was a small country in Africa. I've been sponsoring a child there for the last three year. How much is that? Here, (*Chucking over a pound.*) if thur chinge oot of that gie's a bottle of Irn Bru.

ASSISTANT. (*Tots up items on till.*) Three pounds twenty-seven. (*Pause.*) What are you waiting for?

NESBITT. My surveyor. It seems I've just put in an offer for the place.

ASSISTANT. Look, do you want these things or don't you. I've a queue of people waiting.

NESBITT. Aye, all queuing up to get their pockets dipped. (*To others in queue.*) I don't know what yeez are waiting for, thur

junkies in the alley there, they'll do the same job in half the time with a baseball bat.

ASSISTANT. Look, get out of here, now. If you don't get out, so help me I'll let you have it with this.

He takes a monkey wrench from under the counter, and brandishes it.

NESBITT. Whit yi gonny do with that? Repair me to death? (*Squirting a water pistol at the assistant.*) Gawn, don't be so stupid!

The assistant, dripping, drops the wrench, and flustered, gives a little yap of harassment.

NESBITT. (*To queue.*) 'At's right, it's cabaret time! Don't worry, I've not forgot youse. Watch this!

Nesbitt turns his back, appears to piss into the water pistol to refill it, turns, squirts the queue. There is consternation from all.

NESBITT. (*Standing at door, calls to assistant.*) I'm forty-five tae! Marvellous character, eh? Wonderful spirit!

The monkey wrench whistles past his head.

...Have a nice day! (*Gives single finger gesture.*)

Nesbitt exits. The assistant is shaking with nerves, we see some of the queue behind the counter, consoling him.

SCENE 4. The Nesbitts' living room. Evening.
The Nesbitts' living room as before. Nesbitt enters with a bag. Jamesie, Dodie, Andra leap up in anticipation.

JAMESIE. (*Leaping up.*) Awhaw! Here Rab! Where's my tacos Rab.

DODIE. (*To Nesbitt.*) Got my pakora?

ANDRA. (*Looking at the bag.*) Where's the mignons morceaux?

NESBITT. Never mind all that foreign junk food crap! (*Chucking the bag down.*) Yeez can have some good traditional Scottish junk food and like it!

Smile, Jamesie. Here's a couple of ewes. Yi never know yir luck.

DODIE. (*To Andra and Jamesie.*) What's he got?

ANDRA. (*Holding up a bun.*) Paris buns.

NESBITT. (*Standing in front of television.*) I was reared on Paris buns! Half of Govan was reared on Paris buns! Yi canny afford a dinner! Pamp them full of thae things! Yi know the trouble with youse people, yeez've lost yir national identity!

JAMESIE. I don't like your drift pal. I resent the implication that I don't love Scotland!

DODIE. Aye, I love Scotland better than any of yeez. (*Baring his arm to show 'Bonnie Scotland' tattoo.*) Look, beat that!

ANDRA. (*Exposing bare belly showing 'Scotland for Ever' tattoo.*) ... Beat that!

JAMESIE. (*Lowering trousers to reveal an arse cheek with an 'I Love Scotland' tattoo.*) Beat that!

They all look at Jamesie's bum. Mary enters. She sees Jamesie, Andra and Dodie in full display.

MARY. Aye, very nice. But I'd sooner have the Men of Texas.

They cover themselves happily.

Look Rab, guess what, we've got a lend of a cottage. We can all have a weekend in Ardlui, what'd yi think?

NESBITT. Ardlui, eh? I don't know about that, eh Jamesie?

JAMESIE. No, no way Rab. We're patriots. There's no way we're going to Wales.

NESBITT. Exactly.

They hug each other.

MARY. Ardlui's up Loch Lomond.

Andra and Dodie suppress a snigger. Nesbitt and Jamesie realise they've made a faux pas. They remain frozen, conscious of their cock up.

JAMESIE. (*Sidelong to Nesbitt.*) Egg on face time, Rab.

I sink therefore I am!

I know what you're thinking, how can one man have so much? Limo, chauffeur, good looks...

NESBITT. Brazen it oot, Jamesie. (*To Mary.*) We knew that fine well! We were just being zany, win't we, Jamesie!

JAMESIE. Aye! Wacky kinna guys!

They buddy punch each other wackily.

NESBITT. Jamesie?

JAMESIE. Whit?

NESBITT. Where the hell is Loch Lomond, by the way?

They look at each other quizzically.

SCENE 5. Country roadside. Day.
Further on. The car stops. Inside we see everyone consulting a map.

JAMESIE. It canny be far noo Rab.

NESBITT. Naw. (*He spots someone.*) Look, er a teuchter, I'll go and ask him.

Look at him! If it had hair round it and he could use his dick for a compass he'd find it no bother!

Gets out of the car, shouts to rustic type, who is close by.

NESBITT. (*Calling.*) Hey, haw, Angus! Wee minute.

RUSTIC. Yes, what is it?

NESBITT. (*Showing the rustic a piece of paper.*) We're looking for this drum here. Any idea where it is?

RUSTIC. (*Consulting paper.*) Well let's see ...

A jet screams overhead. They both duck, instinctively.

RUSTIC. ... (*Resurfacing.*) ... Jet.

NESBITT. That a fact. I didnae think it was a cow with a banger up its arse.

RUSTIC. This cottage is on the Glenfalloch Estate. Take the first turn off by the Ministry of Defence road, hard left at the nuclear bunker in the mountain and on past the Wowee Marina and Leisure Complex on the lochside.

NESBITT. (*To audience.*) Nothing like getting away from it all, is there? (*To rustic.*) You're the first teuchter I've met by the way. I bet you'll be aboot a hundred and eight, am I right?

Mary berating me for not helping. But I did my bit. After all, I stopped kipping on the back seat and got out while they were pushing, didn't I?

RUSTIC. I'm thirty-five.

NESBITT. Thirty-five. Gawd, you must've had a hard paper-round, boy. (*He peels back the rustic's lip.*) All the same, you've kept yir ain teeth and everything tae. (*Calls to others.*) Hey, here an Angus, thirty-five, kep all his ain gnashers, look!

Everyone applauds, spontaneously.

NESBITT. (*To rustic, nudging.*) Hey is it true what they say aboot youse crofters and the old sheep dip and that, know what I mean? (*Winks.*) Eh?

RUSTIC. I wouldn't know. I'm a systems analyst. (*He goes.*)

NESBITT. (*To audience.*) Not very friendly roon here are they?

SCENE 6. Country cottage. Day.
A few minutes later.

They arrive outside the door of a rather dilapidated looking cottage, some distance off the road.

It is surrounded by hills, sheep and farmland.

Mary and Ella are at the door, looking at the cottage.

ELLA. Not exactly Balmoral is it, Mary?

MARY. (*Unlocking the front door.*) No still, look at it this way, Ella. At least it's getting us away from the kitchen sink.

She tries to open the door. It won't budge more than a couple of feet.

ELLA. What's blocking the door?

Mary looks behind the door, then back to Ella.

MARY. The kitchen sink.

Mary gives the door a little push. It comes off its hinges and topples over a disused sink in the middle of the floor. The place is a tip inside.

Nesbitt staggers up, carrying a television.

NESBITT. Mary hen. I've got the telly. Where's the nearest plug?

MARY. Better try B & Q.

NESBITT. Whit'd yi mean? Whit'd yi mean?

They all look in at the cottage. A sheep stands, bleating out at them.

NESBITT. A squatter! (*To Jamesie.*) Jamesie, hold this!

He dumps the telly onto Jamesie and picks up a stick.

NESBITT. (*Shouting at sheep.*) Right ya bastard! You're a rug!

JAMESIE. Careful Rab! Yi know what they say! One swipe from a sheep's wing can break yir leg!

We see Nesbitt emerging from the cottage leading the sheep by the scruff of the neck.

NESBITT. (*Shouts to Gash and Burney.*) Hey boys, look! A goat!

Some ground nearby. Gash is cleaning his dark glasses. He calls back.

GASH. (*Calling.*) Aye, yir right there Da! There's nae pulling the wool ower your eyes, eh? (*To Burney.*) What a dildo eh? (*Turns and looks at Burney.*) Haw, what the hell you doing?

Burney stands on a stone wall next to him, one leg raised, poised, vigilant, his hands like little paws held before him, his nose is twitching in the air expectantly.

BURNEY. I smell nookie!

SCENE 7. Country cottage. Day.
Later that day.

Nesbitt and Jamesie are at the back of the house, jackets off, chopping wood on a block.

Nesbitt wields an axe, inexpertly, Jamesie steadies the wood on the block. An old wooden hut is nearby.

JAMESIE. (*Steadying some wood.*) This is the gemme, eh Rab. Chopping wid. Puts yi in touch with yir essential being and that, know.

NESBITT. Bliddy right, Jamesie. A man needs that, by the way.

Physical activity. Puts yi in harmony with nature and that, know? (*Lifting axe.*) Yi right?

JAMESIE. (Steadying wood.) Right y'are, Rab.

NESBITT. Bugger this. I'm choking for a pint, are you not?

JAMESIE. Aye, but we're in the middle of naewhere, Rab. Where'll we fun a pub oot here?

NESBITT. (*Holding up hand reverentially.*) I do not seek, I find.

Nesbitt goes down on his knees, puts his ear to the ground, listens. Having done so he sits up and points.

NESBITT. (*Pointing.*) That way, mile and a half. Free house. Microwave pies and dart board.

JAMESIE. Allow you, Rab. These are the ancient skills that'll die oot with oor generation. But what aboot the lassies? They'll not let us go till we've fun wid for the fire!

Nesbitt gives a superior cough. He leans against the wooden hut. It collapses into pieces.

JAMESIE. It's true what they say, Rab. It's intelligence that separates men from the animals.

NESBITT. Bliddy right. Now let's away and make beasts of wurselves!

JAMESIE & NESBITT. (*Together.*) Hull-oo!

They hurry off, disappearing into the distance, across a field, running. We hear them shout as they run.

JAMESIE. This is brilliant in't it, Rab! Makes yi feel glad to be alive!

NESBITT. Well I widnae go quite that far, Jamesie.

Nesbitt shoots Jamesie, cowboy style, with an imaginary gun.

Jamesie shoots back, making childlike shooting noises. They slap their sides, as if riding horses.

We see them distantly.

I can remember when all this was factories.

The ear splitting roar of a passing military jet drowns their jollity and shadows them.

SCENE 8. Lochside. Day.
A little later.

A cabin cruiser is moored at the lochside. Gash and Burney are standing close to it. Gash nudges Burney.

GASH. (*Out of side of mouth.*) Yi were right.

He nods in the direction of the cabin cruiser. We see it. On deck a couple of girls are smearing themselves with suntan oil.

BURNEY. (*To Gash.*) Lets get nautical.

They mosey over. Gash calls to them.

GASH. (*Calling.*) Aye, aye, dolls! Shiver me timbers and that!

BURNEY. Aye, then when we've shivered his, we'll come ower there and shiver yours too if yeez like!

GIRL 1. (*To Girl 2.*) Wonder which boat they're from?

GIRL 2. God knows. But their patter's off the ark. Let's skoosh them.

She picks up a trailing hosepipe. Lets Gash and Burney have it with a strong jet of water. Gash and Burney struggle to remain upright against the force.

GIRL 2. Boogie! Ya manky oinks!

The two girls cackle maniacally. Suddenly the water subsides. A firm hand grasps the hosepipe. We see a handsome bastard in a ponytail, called Nicky.

NICKY. (*To girl 2.*) Give me that hose, Lorraine. Remember we're a socialist band. There'll be no skooshing of punters from our yacht.

Gash and Burney, dripping wet, are wiping their clothes.

GASH. (*To Burney.*) Haw, is that no thae self righteous bastards we saw playing up at Barrowland?

BURNEY. Which one? All Scottish bands are self righteous.

Cut back to yacht.

GIRL 2. (*Having had hosepipe removed.*) Och Nicky, surely socialism can still be fun?

NICKY. We're the kings of Celtic rock. No fun on a Sunday.

SCENE 9. Pub. Day.
Trendy country pub. Stuffed animals and mounted deer heads around the walls, books on shelves, barmen in kilts. Some touristy climbers sit about.

A local sits at the bar.

We find Nesbitt and Jamesie, pints in hand, waxing expansively.

JAMESIE. This is the gemme, eh Rab? I mean this is the real Scotland! A land of Olafs in hiking boots. Of stuffed nappers roon the walls!

(*To local.*) Yi awright, Angus?

LOCAL. Bugger off.

JAMESIE. Don't you tell me to bugger aff. I'll take that crook and ram it up yir cheviot valley!

BARMAN. (*Southern English accent.*) Hoi! No aggravation! We don't want the tourists getting a bad impression of Scotland, right?

NESBITT. Oh aye? And tell me, what part of Brigadoon are you from, Hamish?

BARMAN. Dagenham. I bought this place a couple of years ago. It was going for a song.

LOCAL. (*Moving along bar.*) Aye, a lament more like.

BARMAN. (*To Nesbitt and Jamesie.*) So unless you moderate your language, you can leave now.

JAMESIE. It's oor bliddy language. We'll do what the hell we want with it!

NESBITT. (*Calming Jamesie.*) Easy, Jamesie. We don't want to start any bother, they might bar us from the Ceilidh tonight.

JAMESIE. I don't care. He's claimed!

NESBITT. And besides, yi know what these wee places are like. If they don't like yi roon here they don't do normal stuff like bushwhack yi on yir way to the lavvies. They take yi up the braes and shag yi and eat yi.

JAMESIE. Well if yi put it like that. (*Tugging his forelock politely to the local.*) Nae offence, pal, heedrum hodrum!

NESBITT. (*Leading Jamesie away.*) 'Mon Jamesie, we'll drink where wur welcome! (*To a climber as they exit.*) Awright Sven, be cauld up the mountains this weather, eh?

CLIMBER. (*Scandinavian accent.*) Yes. That's why we're wearing crampons.

NESBITT. Crampons?

(*To audience.*) I think that's taking this new man carry on a bit far, don't youse?

SCENE 10. Country cottage. Evening.
Mary and Ella sitting. Inside the cottage. Faces fuming, dressed for a night out. Nesbitt and Jamesie are standing, quite contrite.

ELLA. Will youse two get hep. Youse're supposed to be taking us to thon Ceilidh the night.

JAMESIE. First things first, Ella. We canny go jigging on an empty belly. Any chance of some scran?

ELLA. Certainly Jamesie. Yir dinner's in the saucepan.

JAMESIE. Where's the saucepan?

ELLA. In the suitcase.

Jamesie walks over to suitcase, lifts the lid, takes out a saucepan with an unopened tin in it.

JAMESIE. Rab, lookit!

NESBITT. And we went to all the bother of getting yeez firewood!

MARY. (*Pointing to fireplace .*) Aye, thanks a bunch!

Gash walks away disconsolate, after being beaten to the last ribbed condom in the packet.

We see the fireplace. Large planks of shed wood project from the grate.

JAMESIE. Well, could yeez not have lit the bloody thing? Coupla sticks or two dry stones would've done it.

ELLA. (*Prodding Jamesie's groin with some bellows.*) You took the only dry stones with yi, pal.

JAMESIE. Pack that in you! That is a slur!

NESBITT. Awright, keep the heid! Look, we'll away and get washed. Where's the bathroom, Mary?

MARY. The bathroom? Ha! The bathroom's in the toilet, Rab.

NESBITT. Awright, smart arse. Where's the toilet, well?

MARY. (*Pointing out of window.*) Oot there. It's called the Cairngorms!

NESBITT. (*To audience.*) Walked right into that yin, din't I?

SCENE 11. Bushes. Night.
We see some isolated bushes. The voices of Nesbitt and Jamesie are coming from behind them.

JAMESIE. (*Out of vision.*) Tell yi wan thing, Rab. Yi learn something aboot yirself, being at one with nature, don't yi?

NESBITT. Yi do that, Jamesie. Tell yi another thing yi learn an' all.

JAMESIE. What's that?

NESBITT. Never wipe yir arse with a jaggy nettle. Jeez! I know what yi mean though. I'm beginning to realise thur that much aboot Scotland I just didnae know.

JAMESIE. Aye.

A whistle blows piercingly in their ears. It startles them.

NESBITT. (*Shouts.*) God Almighty!

A shout: 'Forward.'

The bushes suddenly disperse, leaving Jamesie and Nesbitt in full view, their trousers around their ankles, clinging to each other, terrified.

We realise that the bushes have been soldiers in camouflage. The bush with the whistle returns to Jamesie and Nesbitt and offers a word of explanation.

BUSH. NATO Forces. Land manoeuvres!

JAMESIE. (*All atremble, to Nesbitt.*) I see what yi mean, Rab. I see what yi mean.

SCENE 12. Ceilidh. Night.

At a Ceilidh. A teuchter band is playing gently. People are sitting drinking, waiting for the jigging to start, or hanging about talking in a loose radius around the bar.

Mary and Ella are sitting at a table. Looking awkward.

MARY. Yi feel that awkward sitting here. What the hell's keeping them. How could they not have got dressed in the hoose?

ELLA. (*Mimicking Jamesie.*) 'I want it to be a surprise, Ella.' Anyway, I think we're safe enough. We've not got what the men roon here are looking for.

MARY. What's that?

ELLA. Four legs and a tail.

Ella indicates to a large red bearded teuchter, pint in hand. He is winking at a dog, making provocative lip licking gestures.

MARY. In the namea God!

ELLA. I know, it's disgusting. And it's not even a pedigree.

MARY. Not there! (*Indicating.*) There!

ELLA. (*Seeing something.*) Oh my God!

MARY. Dive, Ella, dive!

They shrink in their seats.

Nesbitt and Jamesie have appeared at the door. They're wearing kilts. This is the only concession to Highland dress they've made. Short socks, trainers prevail. Jamesie wears cycling shorts under his kilt.

NESBITT. (*Waving.*) Mary, Mary! (*Swinging and flaunting kilt.*)
Pure gallus, eh doll!

ELLA. Too late, they've seen us.

Jamesie and Nesbitt arrive at the table.

JAMESIE. (*To Ella, in response.*) Aye, and it gets better tae. Show
her Rab!

Nesbitt lifts his kilt. He's wearing a sporran inside the kilt.

NESBITT. (*Calls out to everyone.*) It's a lot more fun worn inside
than oot, I'll tell yi!

*He gives the sporran a wiggle. The teuchter band strike that chord
which means 'Time to dance'.*

NESBITT & JAMESIE. (*Together.*) Hull-ooo.

They begin to do the 'slosh'.

MARY. (*To Ella, glaring at them.*) Fair come on since the year of
culture, hin't they?

Mary and Ella hide their faces, mortified.

*Cut to quick clip of the band in action to establish a passage of
time.*

*A little later on Nicky, the handsome bastard, is standing,
unobtrusively, at the rear of the hall, enjoying the music.*

*Girl 1 is with him. He's signing a couple of casual autographs
when Gash and Burney happen to drop by. Nicky spies them.*

NICKY. (*To Gash and Burney. Says the Teuchter for* 'Hello',
then...) You enjoying yourselves. Lovely melody isn't it?

BURNEY. Nuh. It's pish.

GASH. Shuttit you! (*To Nicky.*) He's got to say that, you're into
Celtic rock, you'll stick a disco drum track and a synth under it
and pamp it on yir next LP.

NICKY. (*Smirking.*) 'LP.' Listen, we're not like other bands, we've
kept our integrity. We believed in Scottish socialism right at the
beginning.

Why not beautify your garden with 'Rent-a-gnome'.

GIRL 1. Yes. And now that we're millionaires we believe in it even more!

NICKY. (*To girl 1.*) Shuttit you!

BURNEY. (*Thrusting piece of paper in front of Nicky.*) I'm glad to hear it. That's dead reassuring. Gonny gie's yir autograph well?

NICKY. (*Taking paper.*) Sure. (*Signing.*) What is this? A pledge of my commitment to reinstating clause 84? (*Smirks.*)

GASH. Nuh. It's a tic form from Rumbelows. You've just signed as guarantor on a CD player!

NICKY. (*Shouting after them.*) Haw! Haw! Ya pair of scabby fu...

Gash and Burney scarper.

Later. Cut to the table. Mary, Ella, Jamesie, Nesbitt. Jamesie is drunk. He is singing.

JAMESIE. 'For these are my mountains ...' (*He sees a female dancer nearby, and starts to get friendly.*) Awright doll? That you stripping the willow? If yi want I'll strip it for yi. Ha!

NESBITT. (*Calling.*) Haw, Cotter, sober up! Steady the McBuff for God's sake!

JAMESIE. Sorry Rab! Sorry, sorry! Nae offence, Ella hen. It's just I've fun my spiritual home, know? Among the Anguses. The Anguses are oor brars, Rab!

NESBITT. Awright, awright. Sit down, yir making an arse of yirself.

Music starts to play. Jamesie's ears prick up.

JAMESIE. Rab! Listen! They're playing oor anthem! Floower of Scoatlin! Let's hear it for the teuchters! A struggle on their soil, is a struggle on my soil! (*Moved, raising glass.*) Ich Bin Ein Sheepshagger!

A red bearded teuchter overhears.

RED BEARD. Who are you calling a sheepshagger?

He lands Jamesie one. Jamesie falls backwards into a tableful of the Scandinavian climbers they met earlier in the pub.

Honest doll, I love yi for yir mind!

CLIMBER 1. (*To Jamesie, irate.*) You are a hooligan!

CLIMBER 2. (*Wiping drink off himself.*) Yes! Why don't you get back to your tenements!

NESBITT. (*To climbers.*) Who the bliddy hell'd you think you're talking to? Just coz he's committed the crime of being Scottish! See youse people? Yeez think yeez are something just coz yeez've got boots on yeez the price of a three piece suite! Jamesie? Jamesie?

He looks about. Jamesie's gone. The barman from earlier, now in full Highland dress, returns from the door, dusting his hands.

BARMAN. (*To Nesbitt.*) You wanna watch him. It's people like him that give Scots a bad name!

NESBITT. Aye. And don't you ever forget it!

He picks up a lump of haggis, rams it into the barman's mouth.

NESBITT. (*To audience.*) Well if yir gonny get the name of it, yi might as well do it. Know what I mean? (*Hurrying to door calling.*) Jamesie! Jamesie!

SCENE 13. On a mountainside. Evening.
Just afterwards, outside on the mountainside. Nesbitt is pursuing Jamesie.

NESBITT. (*Giving up, he stops, puffed.*) Jamesie! Jamesie! (*To audience.*) 'These are my mountains,' eh? Aye, and yeez can bliddy well have them if yeez want them! Most of them are nothing but lids for nuclear dustbins anyway! Yi can just see the equation in the Westminster nappers, can't yi? 'Oh the Jocks?' All their industry's deid on its feet, well the cruddy animals are gonny pay for their giros somehow. Mon we'll dump all wur radioactive keech all ower their front room. Bonnie purple heather is it? The bloody stuff glows in the dark up here! Mother country is it? Some bliddy mother! Major's poking her up the old Glencoe with his nuclear rod and her ain weans are hinging from her belly squeezing her tits like bagpipes.

One of the sadder sights of the countryside – a dead marriage by the side of the road.

World exclusive! We reveal the bastard sons of Abba!

He points down the hillside to the cruiser in the jetty.

'Hullo Jock, welcome to Tin Pan Alley, brought your ethnic tradition with you? Good. Here's a hundred K, get yourself a ponytail and a misty eyed expression.'

We hear runrig type music coming from the cruiser.

NESBITT. Listen to that eh? Brigadoon for the nineties. If music be the food of love, Celtic rock is its colostomy bag. Scottish culture is it? Don't talk to me. Never mind a drunk man looks at a thistle. The whole bloody country wants to take a good swatch in a mirror!

He sees a solitary thistle and glares at it.

(*To thistle.*) Whit you looking at?

He uproots the thistle with a tug, shouts at it.

. . . Bastard!

Suddenly the earth moves under his feet. A camouflaged military man, the same one with the bush earlier, pokes his head up through a flap in the land.

MILITARY MAN. Oh, sorry Jock. Manoeuvres.

NESBITT. I'll give yi manoeuvres, boy. I'll manoeuvre my toe right up yir archibald and do collateral damage to yir colon! (*Closing turf lid on military man.*) . . . Gawn, get doon that strategic cesspit where yi belong! It's high time the silent majority opened wur yaps, bared wur teeth and put wur bliddy foot down!

He slams his foot down hard on the lid, trapping the military man's fingers.

. . . That's for Dounreay!

Another stomp, another yell.

. . . That's for Hunterston!

Another stomp, another yell.

. . . And that's for . . .

He fumbles in his mind.

Another stomp, another yell.

. . . And that's for 9–3 at Wembley in 1961!

(*To audience.*) Ah well, that's Scottish history avenged. I think I'll just take a walk across the water back to Nesbitt Castle noo.

A peel of thunder roars. Nesbitt jumps.

(*Looking up to sky.*) . . . No offence, bigman. Just joking.

The heavens open, Nesbitt opens the turf flap and waves a white hankie.

. . . Hey Percy! Graham Taylor okay. Yi got room for one more in the dugoot?

(*To audience.*) It's not a defeat yi understand, just a strategic withdrawal. (*Climbs down into the hole.*) Gazza and that! John Mills!

Thunder, lightning, rain, continue.

Seen this pair, Jamesie? I'm not saying time's been cruel to them but they're wearing second bras roon the back to stop their arses from bouncing off the pavement.

SCENE 14. On the mountainside. Morning.
Bright, sunny, cloudless, morning. We get a glance at the beautiful rolling hills.

Music: Grieg. 'Morning'.

Nesbitt with his head sticking out of the opened flap in the ground, his jacket off, a knotted hankie on his head.

NESBITT. (*To audience.*) Did yeez see that there? Did yeez clock that. That's the Scotland boy. Got the lot. Rolling hills. Friendly natives like myself. So where's yir Skegness noo, ya bams!

A shadow falls over him. He looks up. Mary skites him.

NESBITT. Morning, Mary hen.

MARY. Don't morning me. Where the hell've you been all night, fella?

NESBITT. Doon there in hell's kitchen playing aboot with the slot machines.

MARY. What slot machines?

NESBITT. Well it's either that or I've just blown up half of Russia. How?

MARY. Coz Cotter didnae come hame last night. He's been up there stoating aboot the mountain.

NESBITT. Whaaat? There was a thunderstorm last night and it was bitter cold. Surely even Cotter's got enough sense to get in oot the rain?

They look at each other.

NESBITT. Come on! (*Climbing out of the hole.*) We better get up that mountain rescue!

SCENE 15. On the mountainside. Day.
A little later.

Near the foot of the mountain. The climber types from the pub are about to begin an ascent. The barman is leading them. All wear appropriate weather, safety gear.

BARMAN. (*To climbers.*) Of course even at this time of year the summit can be freezing. So it's good to see you're all wearing the appropriate...

CLIMBER 1. (*Interrupts, pointing.*) Look, what is that?

They all look. We see two crofters, some distance away, carrying a long pole over both their shoulders.

CLIMBER 2. It must be some sort of creature dead from exposure.

The two crofters are passing. We see in the middle of the pole, frozen, snow bound, Jamesie, curled and tied in the foetal position. Ice has formed on his features. He is blue in colour.

CROFTER 1. (*To barman, in passing.*) We saw through the binoculars. He was standing cursing and shaking his fist on the mountain top. He's mad! Absolutely mad!

JAMESIE. (*To barman, in passing.*) Climbing is it? Take a good look, Percy. This is Govan climbing gear, pal. A T-shirt, ten fags and a sarcastic expression.

Nesbitt turns up with Mary.

NESBITT. Jamesie! Jamesie! Yi awright, my man?

JAMESIE. In the pink, Rab. Just wan thing. (*For the benefit of the barman and climbers.*) Gonny take aff this jacket for me? I'm boiling!

NESBITT. (*To audience.*) Hear that, eh? Pure radio rental! (*To Jamesie.*) Put it there, my man! Put it there!

He grasps Jamesie's hand. We hear a pinging sound.

JAMESIE. That digit, Rab! Get that finger!

NESBITT. Sorry Jamesie, sorry. (*Retrieves finger, sees climbers' look of horrified fascination.*) Whit youse looking at? Scumballs ya bas! (*Gesturing with Jamesie's finger.*) Get it right up yeez. Get it right up yeez! 'Mon Mary, hen.

The climbers step back, alarmed.

MARY. (*To climbers.*) Cheerio! (*Goes. Comes back.*) Oh, and haste ye back!

She looks. The climbers are some distance away, legging it.

... Queer lot, foreigners.

She shrugs and goes.

SCENE 16. Country road. Day.
Music: something with a mood of the Highlands.

Nesbitt is at the wheel of the car.

NESBITT. See when yi get right down to it. Yir country's like yir ain fizzog. It might be a run doon, pockmarked, drink-ridden, eyesore, but yir stuck with it, so yi might as well try and love it.

Someone shouts. A young boy, suitcase in hand, is trying to cadge a lift.

The car stops.

BOY. Hey pal, any chance of a hurl?

NESBITT. Aye, sure. Where yi gawn?

BOY. (*Slinging his case into the back of the car.*) Ach, there's nothing up here. I'm going to Glesga to join the army.

NESBITT. (*To audience.*) But it's hell of a bliddy hard sometimes.

Boy goes to get into car.

... Haw, where'd yi think yir gawn? Get back there and push with all the rest!

We see then that Mary, Ella, Gash and Burney are pushing the car. Nesbitt's point of view. He stands, saluting the hills.

NESBITT. (*To the hills.*) I shall return!

The car begins to roll, freewheeling downhill. Nesbitt recedes into the distance, shouting oaths.

We hear highland music.

Nice to get some fresh country air into yir lungs, isn't it?

EPISODE THREE

That's Entertainment

CAST LIST

RAB C. NESBITT · Gregor Fisher
ANDRA · Brian Pettifer
DODIE · Iain McColl
JUDGE · Iain Cuthbertson
McGURN · Maurice Roeves
LAWYER · Paul Young
BIMBO · David McKay
JAMESIE COTTER · Tony Roper
BURNEY · Eric Cullen
GASH · Andrew Fairlie
MARY NESBITT · Elaine C. Smith
ELLA COTTER · Barbara Rafferty
DOUGIE · Charlie Sim
NORRIE · John Kazek
WAITRESS · Mandy Matthews
TRACEY · Caroline Paterson
PSYCHOLOGIST · Tamara Kennedy
INSPECTOR · Paul Heasman

SCENE 1. Waste ground. Day.
Waste ground. A nice day. Nesbitt is standing with something on a lead. We don't see what it is yet.

NESBITT. (*To audience.*) Yeez awright? Some weather, eh? This is me, got the jaicket off, trying to get a wee touch of skin cancer. Maybes noise up the DSS, know? Make them think I can afford a holiday abroad.

He throws a stick.

(*To thing on lead.*) ... Fetch, Shep! Shep, fetch!

(*No movement from the lead.*) (*To audience.*) Old Shep there, my new pet. I've got a wife and two weans so it's nice to get some affection for a change. (*To thing on lead.*) In't that right, boy? (*A slight twitch on the lead.*) Frisky wee swine, so he is. Takes after his auld Da here, know what I mean. (*To lead.*) Yir a stud, in't yi! Yir a sex machine!

He chucks another stick.

(*Shouts.*) ... Fetch...!

Camera pulls out to reveal that Nesbitt has a canary on a string. A small pile of unretrieved sticks lie ahead.

(*To audience.*) I know what yir thinking – mental Govan bastard! Bliddy right. And don't youse ever forget it!

A fierce tug comes from the lead. They move off. (*To audience.*) He's a heidstrong wee swine, so he is! Actually, I thought aboot getting a dog. But dogs is noisy critters. And they're aye doing their business in public. Not civilised like us humans, know?

Singing can be heard as Nesbitt strolls along. We hear 'Put youra sweet lips a leettle closer to ri phoneeeee...'

It's Andra and Dodie. They're in a phone box, pissing.

NESBITT. (*Seeing them.*) Awright there boys. Lovely day eh?

ANDRA. (*Sniffily.*) Might be.

NESBITT. Aye! Kinna makes yi feel good to be alive, know?

DODIE. Well I widnae want to go that far, Rab.

ANDRA. Aye. Whit kinna talk's that in Govan?

NESBITT. What'd yi mean, I was just smiling!

DODIE. Aye, that's how it starts. First yir smiling, then yir drinking Aqua Libras, next thing yi'll be shacked up in a beach house in Malibu with Kim Basinger!

ANDRA. Aye, that's you all over, Nesbitt. Yi'd sooner sleep with a Hollywood sex goddess than pish in a phone box with yir pals!

NESBITT. What? No! Never! (To audience.) Whit am I talking aboot? I'd sooner sleep with a Ninja Turtle than hing aboot with them.

ANDRA. Aye. Yi know your trouble, Nesbitt. Yiv turned normal!

NESBITT. Don't you call me names boys! Who you calling *normal*! I was deranged while you were still lying in yir cot using yir wullie as a tent pole wondering what to do with yir hands! *Normal* is it? *Normal*? I've had electric shock therapy! I'm stoating aboot talking to myself with a canary on a lead! Are you trying to tell me that's *normal*?

DODIE. It is in Govan.

NESBITT. Aye, well fair enough, yiv got a point there. (To audience.) That's the trouble roon here. It's not enough yi keep yir feet on the grun, yiv got to keep yir heid in the gutter as well. (To Dodie.) Talking of shite, where is Cotter the day anyway?

DODIE. He's up the barber's getting his highlights done.

NESBITT. Well that's good share news for Dulux. Eh Andra?

ANDRA. Don't try and sook in with me. Yi think yir a big man just coz yiv got a split personality, but Young Young McGurn's more mental than you any day of the week.

NESBITT. Ach away and lie in yir pish.

(To audience.) Sorry about that wee indelicacy there, but sometimes I prefer to use the verbal bludgeon rather than the rapier, know what I mean? 'Mon Shep.

SCENE 2. Courtroom. Day.
A judge is sitting at the bench. A prisoner is in the dock. A lawyer is defending him. A policeman is in attendance.

JUDGE. John William Pure Mad Mental, intae yir boady, Simpson Craig Gemmell, chib the bam, ribracker, no real, young Rebel ya bass, St John McGurn. You are a thug and a hooligan.

MCGURN. 'At's right! Gie a dog a bad name!

JUDGE. Quiet!

LAWYER. My Lord, my client's character has undergone a change since his youthful criminal days. Fatherhood has given him a sense of responsibility.

MCGURN. Bliddy right. (*Points to gallery.*) 'At's my offspring up there. Awright, Bimbo son?

BIMBO. (*Calls down.*) Aye, awright Da! (*Making macho groin gesture.*) Get right intae rum!

JUDGE. Quiet.

LAWYER. (*Hastening on.*) My Lord, my client has even written you a full and frank apology for the crimes he has committed against society.

JUDGE. Where is it then?

LAWYER. He ate it, My Lord.

JUDGE. Ate it?

LAWYER. Yes, but even that is a significant behavioural advance.

JUDGE. Why?

LAWYER. He had threatened to eat *you*, My Lord.

MCGURN. 'At is right, by the way. My behaviour is advanced. Not only do I love my neighbour, but gie me half a chance, I'll eat the bastard as well. (*To policeman next to him.*) Whit you looking at? You want devoured?

He pulls off the policeman's hat and tears a bite out of it.

POLICEMAN. (*Shocked.*) Aaaahhhh!

From the gallery. Grotesque looking bears cheer, stomp feet, throw down handfuls of raw mince.

JUDGE. Silence! Any more of this gothic horror show and I'll clear

the chamber! (*To the lawyer.*) Mr Horswill, what on earth is wrong with this client of yours?

LAWYER. I would plead for leniency, My Lord. My client has a human problem.

JUDGE. What sort of human problem?

LAWYER. Well he isn't really human, he's from Wine Alley. In addition his teenage daughter has been involved with an older man, My Lord. This has caused him some distress.

MCGURN. That is correct. And when I'm distressed, *I eat people.* I mean it's only fair, in't it?

Cries of support come from the gallery.

JUDGE. McGurn, I'm going to fine you for your offences and allow you time to pay. You are outside society. People like you have not so much escaped the social work safety net as chewed your way through it. But I warn you, come before me again and you will go to prison for a very long time. You may go.

MCGURN. (*Clenches fist victoriously.*) Yeeeeeeesssssss!

He tears off the policeman's hat again, and tears another chunk out of it.

(*To policeman.*) Any lip and I'll have yir nose for a pudding! (*Calling.*) Bimbo son! Yi got the transport?

BIMBO. (*Pointing.*) Here it comes noo, Da!

A motor-cycle, ridden by a bear, enters the court. McGurn kicks off the bear and jumps on.

MCGURN. (*Calls.*) Got my chib, son?

BIMBO. (*Chucking him a sword.*) 'Er it's Da!

McGurn catches the sword by the handle, brandishes it, to the delight of the bears.

MCGURN. (*Screaming.*) Yeeessss!

He travels a couple of feet, then addresses lawyer.

Jamesie Cotter – the thinking woman's dildo.

... Oh by the way, big man, well done! (*Pumps lawyer's hand.*) A victory for common sense! (*Turns.*) Hey, Bimbo son!

BIMBO. Whit Da?

MCGURN. Whit do we know aboot this walking dinner that's whapping the meat up oor Tracey?

BIMBO. Not much Da. I just got a swatch at him disappearing oot the kitchen window.

MCGURN. I see. And whit did he look like?

BIMBO. I don't know Da. He was a kinna pathetic looking middle-aged grunter. Oh aye, he was wearing white training shoes.

SCENE 3. Street/underpass. Day.
We see a pair of white shoes. The wearer is placing one, very deliberately, into a small puddle.

JAMESIE. (*Out of view.*) Look Rab. Yi watching?

NESBITT. I'm watching.

Jamesie, the owner of the shoes, treads his foot on the pavement, leaving a clear wet imprint.

JAMESIE. I love a shoe that leaves a good imprint, Rab. See when I die, I want them to say that of me – some men climb Everest, some men write symphonies, but Jamesie Cotter left a good imprint when he stood in a puddle – know.

NESBITT. A proud boast, Jamesie. And the way we're going they'll be saying it about yi a damn sight quicker than yi bargained for.

JAMESIE. Whit'd yi mean?

NESBITT. (*Indicates ahead.*) Careful. We're entering Apache country.

They're near a darkened underpass. Nesbitt points to graffiti on a wall. It reads 'McGurn territiry. We will kill and eat you.'

JAMESIE. Look at that, Rab. It's people like that that's gieing violence a bad name nowadays.

NESBITT. Aye, it kinna makes yi nostalgic for the old days. You know, when all yi got when yi staggered drunk through the underpass was maybes a routine hatchet through the heid or some junkie using yir arse as a dartboard.

JAMESIE. Aye, thur nae morals nooawadays. Just as well we brung the skateboard, eh Rab.

NESBITT. Aye. This might be an ambush. Pamp the fake carry oot on it to keep them occupied and we'll get hep for the chicken run.

JAMESIE. (*Doing so.*) Right Rab. Ready when you are.

NESBITT. Okay. Go!

Jamesie pushes the skateboard hard down the slope of the underpass into the darkness. They dart out into the street, dodging cars, to collect it at the other end.

Nesbitt and Jamesie in the street dodging cars and shouting. 'Gawn … Get tae …' They kick bumpers, gesticulate etc. Finally they make it to the other side.

NESBITT. (*To audience.*) I'll tell yi something. Yi don't half need a clear head to be a drunk nooadays. (*To Jamesie.*) Is it here yet, Jamesie?

JAMESIE. Here it comes noo Rab.

The skateboard reappears. The carry out is gone.

NESBITT. Allow us, eh Jamesie? We outflanked them there with wur superior intelligence, eh?

JAMESIE. Aye! Wait a minute there's a note attached.

NESBITT. What's it say?

JAMESIE. (*Reading.*) 'While youse are reading this, thinking youse have outflanked us, we are up your hooses blagging yir microwaves and videos. Best wishes, The McGurns.'

NESBITT. Huh! That old trick. We're not gonny fall for that, are we Jamesie?

JAMESIE. I think we are, Rab.

NESBITT. Bliddy right. 'Mon, let's jildy!

JAMESIE. Just a wee minute, Rab.

Jamesie steps his foot into a puddle, to try out the imprint again. Nesbitt boots his arse.

NESBITT. Never mind that! (*Booting him again.*) 'Mon, get yir arse in gear!

JAMESIE. I'm gawn, I'm gawn!

They run off up the road.

SCENE 4. The Nesbitts' living room. Day.

The Nesbitts' living room. After a battle. Smoke rises from the odd bit of smouldering furniture. Gash and Burney lean on brooms, exhausted, spent in the defence of the Nesbitt realm. Nesbitt pets Shep, places him in his cage.

NESBITT. (*To Burney.*) Broke in? Whit'd yi mean broke in?

BURNEY. I mean they stormed the door Da, in the traditional McGurn way.

GASH. (*Holding up piece of door with a hole in it.*) Aye, heid first. We tried to fight them aff Da. But they had superior technological hardware.

BURNEY. (*Shows a stick with a nail in it.*) Aye, the Govan Cruise missile. Not only does it leave the building standing, but it blags it and leaves a turd on the carpet as well. (*Points.*) Look, Da.

A turd. But we don't see it.

NESBITT. (*Looks at it.*) Mockit bastards!

MARY. (*Enters, mop in hand.*) Aye, and you can clean that up Rab. I'm not going near it. I feel sullied.

BURNEY. But we are sullied. We're Nesbitts.

NESBITT. (*Skites him.*) Shuttit you! Yir maw's right. Youse boys don't realise the kinna world we're living in the day. The kinna things me and yir maw try to protect yi from. Things like violence, drugs...

GASH. ... Work.

NESBITT. Exactly. The world's not the place it used to be. I mean, I might be a parasite. But there's a strain of superparasite going about these days that makes us Nesbitts look like the Royal Family.

MARY. Och come on, we're not that bad.

NESBITT. Fair enough, but yi get the point. I mean look at this. (*He picks up a wire mesh thing that you get in a chip pan.*) They're away with wur chip pan, I ask yi. Whit manner of vermin would do that? In scum terms that's like unplugging a life-support machine.

BURNEY. It could've been worse Da. They could've got away with the family allowance book.

NESBITT. No chance. That's in my personal safe deposit box.

He rummages his fingers into his head bandage and produces from behind it, the family allowance book.

GASH. Ugh. That's disgusting.

MARY. You think so? He used to keep it stuffed up his ar—

NESBITT. 'At's enough! This is a family crisis here! Wur whole value system's under attack. I mean whit are they picking on us for?

GASH. It's just wur Donald Duck Da. Young young McGurn got off with a suspended sentence. So they're celebrating by having a hoosewarming.

BURNEY. (*Holding up a smouldering curtain.*) Aye, and oors was the hoose they chose to warm.

MARY. (*Snatching curtain.*) Don't remind me!

JAMESIE. (*Appearing at the door.*) And not only yours Rab. (*With trembling lip.*) Look at that.

He holds up two handfuls of charcoaled waste, from which two laces can just be discerned.

NESBITT. (*Looks, horrified.*) They didnae?

JAMESIE. Aye, Rab. They stepped on my blue suede shoes!

BURNEY. (*Furtively, to Jamesie.*) They'll step on a lot more than that if they fun oot about you and Tracey McGurn.

JAMESIE. (*Gives him an ankle tap with his foot.*) Shuttit you!

ELLA. (*Entering.*) What was that?

JAMESIE. Nothing Ella hen. I was just saying it's high time sumhin was done about thae McGurns!

ELLA. True enough. But what's a hinging dewdrop like you gonny do? Ring their doorbell, fill yir troosers and sicken them to death?

JAMESIE. Did yi hear that Rab? That is a slur. They've got a low opinion of you!

NESBITT. Leave me oot of it. It's your troosers.

MARY. Ella's right Rab. We canny go on living in fear like this. If the polis'll not do anything, youse'll have to.

NESBITT. Us?

MARY & ELLA. (*Together.*) Youse!

NESBITT. Fair enough. (*To Jamesie.*) Hey Jamesie, if we're gonny fight we better stop off at the chemist first.

JAMESIE. What for, some vaseline for wur eyebrows?

NESBITT. No, some Pampers for wur arses.

Nesbitt adjusts his trousers, discreetly.

SCENE 5. The McGurns' house. Day.
Later, Nesbitt and Jamesie outside the McGurns' house. They're preparing themselves.

NESBITT. Right, Jamesie. Think of the good old days. Razor fights. Blue Murder. 'No mean city'. We came up the hard way!

JAMESIE. I'm with yi, big man. Let's get him!

They walk 'hard' to the door of the house. Nesbitt knocks on the door. It falls inwardly. Bimbo stands defiantly.

BIMBO. Whit is it?

JAMESIE. (*Acting hard.*) Your Da in, kid?

BIMBO. (*Shouts.*) Hey Da!

Election time. And the Govan nationalist candidate takes time out to make a subtle point.

MCGURN. (*Appears in vest, eating a leg of something raw.*) Aye, whit is it. Whit do youse two want?

JAMESIE. (*In a soft voice.*) Eh, have you ever thought of letting God enter your life?

Nesbitt skites him.

NESBITT. (*To McGurn.*) Look you. We're from ower the road. Did you just break into oor hooses?

MCGURN. Aye, what of it?

JAMESIE. Nothing, just as long as we know. Cheery by the now!

Jamesie turns to go, Nesbitt stops him.

NESBITT. (*To Jamesie.*) Wait there you! (*To McGurn.*) See you, I don't like your type. If you've got to tea leaf, at least tea leaf offa them that can afford it, don't thieve affa them that's as skint as yirself. But you'll not will yi, coz people like you are nuhing but mobile appetites. The living embodiment of the rottweiler culture.

MCGURN. 'At where yir wrang. I don't have a rottweiler.

BIMBO. Not any more.

NESBITT. What happened to it?

MCGURN. (*Showing the leg that he's eating.*) I'm eating it. (*Leans in close, breathing on Nesbitt.*) And if I lay hons on the gink that's nipping my Tracey, I'll eat him too.

NESBITT. (*Swallows.*) What gink?

BIMBO. A pathetic old grunter, in white trainers.

MCGURN. (*Flesh hanging from his teeth.*) Do I make myself clear?

NESBITT. Perfectly. In' that right, Jamesie? Jamesie?

Jamesie's gone, nowhere to be seen.

MCGURN. (*To Bimbo, suspicious.*) Bimbo son, get me that footprint from off the kitchen window sill.

BIMBO. Right Da. Anything else?

MCGURN. Aye. And get me my bib and toothpick.

NESBITT. (*Swallows again, mutters to himself.*) For what we are about to receive . . .

SCENE 6. Street/billboard. Day.

Meanwhile. Further along, outside in the street. Jamesie is standing, lighting a fag, all atremble. Hands shaking. He looks up at a billboard. It has an ad depicting a family tucking into a Sunday joint.

JAMESIE. (*He sees the ad, then tries to light up.*) In the name...

A hand appears on his shoulder, a voice comes from behind.

ANDRA. Awright, Jamesie?

JAMESIE. (*He jumps, yelps.*) Don't eat me, I'm full of gristle!

Jamesie turns around. Andra and Dodie are standing there.

...Oh it's youse. Yi shouldnie sneak up behind a Bar L man, yir liable to get hurtit, know?

ANDRA. (*To Dodie.*) Aye, he could break yir toes when he faints at yir feet.

JAMESIE. You watch it, or you'll get what McGurn's just got. Me and Rab have just marked his card.

DODIE. You squared up to Young Young McGurn! Were yi not feart?

JAMESIE. Not me. Not this kid. Well, not much feart anyway. See yeez.

He turns. Goes.

DODIE. (*Calls to Jamesie.*) How much feart well?

ANDRA. (*To Dodie.*) Oh, I'd say about ... a pint and a quarter.

Dodie nods toward a puddle on the ground. They both look. Jamesie's dampened footsteps guide their eyes toward a damp patch on the back of his trousers as he walks on.

SCENE 7. The McGurns' house. Day.

Meanwhile. Bimbo McGurn and Young Young McGurn kneel at the doorstep outside. They compare Jamesie's distinctive footprint with the one on a piece of rotting window sill that Bimbo has laid alongside. We see that they are the same. Then McGurn looks at Bimbo.

It's hellraiser time at the Govan branch of Stringfellows as Lionel Richie and Raphael from the Ninja Turtles enjoy a cocktail.

MCGURN. (*Tucking in his bib.*) Dinner is served.

SCENE 8. Two Ways pub. Day.
Andra and Dodie are at the bar. Jamesie is sitting, reading a glossy magazine.

Dougie the barman is serving. Norrie, the new barman, stands near Andra and Dodie. Andra and Dodie are watching telly. We see in close up a footage of the burning Kuwaiti oil fields, then a shot of Saddam Hussein smiling.

DODIE. (*Fearfully, tinged with admiration.*) Allow big Saddam, eh? Look at thae eyes. I bet he has no bother getting a single payment oot the DSS.

ANDRA. Aye, fair enough he's maybes a psychopathic despot withoot a shred of human feeling in his body, but he's a man's man, in't he?

DODIE. Right! Hey, maybes we could get him in to push ower the Govan sick children's charity bottle, what'd yi think?

ANDRA. Nah, Saddam's a good nutter, but he's not that good. That honour can only go to a nutter with Govan blood.

Norrie, the new barman, has been listening to this in horrified fascination. We see a shot of him, reacting, then Dougie turns to him, casually, polishing a glass.

DOUGIE. How yi doing, Norrie son? Big change from the psychiatric nursing this, eh?

NORRIE. (*Doubtfully.*) Yi think so?

DODIE. (*To Andra.*) Tell yi what, we'll ask Jamesie, maybes he'll do it.

JAMESIE. (*Having heard this.*) Leave me oot of this. I abhor violence. Thur not enough love in the world.

Nesbitt has entered, with his canary. Jamesie sees him.

. . . In't that right, Rab?

NESBITT. Not enough for you, anyway. The only man ever to be treated up the clinic for friction burns to his wallapur. (*To Dougie.*) See's a pint, Dougie. (*He sees Jamesie reading.*) What's that you're reading, the Vegetarian cookbook?

JAMESIE. Whit'd yi talking aboot? What's with the heavy satire?

NESBITT. Don't come the innocent. You know fine well what I'm talking aboot. Running aboot with Tracey McGurn, a wee lassie half your age! If yi'd a brain as big as yir libido yid have enough bliddy sense to know better!

JAMESIE. That is a slur, Rab. I respect that bint. I love her for her mind.

NESBITT. Aye, and I know why. It's the dirtiest mind in Govan. Now you take my advice and use that excuse for a noddle of yours afore Young Young McGurn uses yir bollock pouch for a bum bag!

DOUGIE. (*Serving up pint to Nesbitt.*) Mind yir language Nesbitt. We don't want trouble in this pub.

Dougie looks to Norrie who does an unconvincing shoulder flex.

NESBITT. I'm trying to stop trouble, in't I? I'm trying to wise up that glaikit article! (*He sees the charity bottle.*) What's this, the sick weans' bottle? I suppose yeez'll be wanting me to push it ower this year as normal?

ANDRA. There's only one pushover in here, Nesbitt. And that's you.

NESBITT. (*Seeing Dodie he says to him . . .*) Jeez, that's great that. How you can still talk with that bolt through yir neck.

ANDRA. (*Stepping from behind Dodie.*) He never said it. I said it.

NESBITT. Hey, it's true what they say – inside every big tit thur a wee tit struggling to get oot.

ANDRA. I used to respect you, Nesbitt. But it's time you moved ower for a bigger man.

NESBITT. (*To Dodie.*) Oh aye? And who might that be like?

Dodie, lest Nesbitt should get the wrong idea, shrinks into a modest semi crouch.

ANDRA. (*Wielding a tumbler.*) Come ahead, Nesbitt!! Young blood rules!

DOUGIE. (*Picking up a baseball bat.*) I'm warning you Nesbitt. Any violence and you're barred!

NESBITT. Relax, I'm not gonny fight anybody.

He strokes his canary.

ANDRA. (*To Nesbitt.*) I don't know who's more yella. You or that thing.

NESBITT. (*To Dougie.*) I mean why should I resort to violence, when I've a wee pet to do that for me. (*To canary.*) Shep, kill!

We see the bird. It has a bandage round its head, à la Nesbitt. It launches itself at Andra's crotch and bites. Andra yells in pain.

Dougie goes to speak, Nesbitt raises a hand to silence.

NESBITT. I know, don't tell me. Cock fighting's illegal.

DODIE. In the name of God what kinna canary is that?

NESBITT. A Govan canary. (*To audience.*) A pit bull canary, know?

ANDRA. Get it aff me! Get if aff!

NESBITT. I don't know what he's moaning at. Most blocks'd pay money to have a burd doing that to them, eh Jamesie?

JAMESIE. Leave me out of it Rab. The mature man outgrows that sexist banter. Now if you'll excuse me, I've a dinner engagement.

Jamesie stands, he's wearing cycling shorts and trainers with huge tongues. They all look at him. Jamesie affects innocent bewilderment.

Whut? Whut? Whut is it? Sumhin wrong?

NESBITT. Didnae realise yi were presenting the Disney Club.

JAMESIE. Look you, Tracey McGurn is a mature, sophisticated wumman and we're going to enjoy a quiet meal in appropriate sophisticated surroundings, awright!

NESBITT. Aye, awright, awright.

Jamesie turns to go. Nesbitt calls after him.

McGurn the cannibal was health conscious – and would only ever eat vegetarians.

NESBITT. Haw, Jive Bunny.

Jamesie turns. Nesbitt chucks something at him.

...Yi forgot yir Mr Wimpy hat!

JAMESIE. Ach...

Jamesie slaps a baseball cap on his head, spins it back to front.

JAMESIE. Grow up!

Jamesie turns on his heel. Andra lets out a moan of pain.

NESBITT. (*To canary.*) 'Mon Shep, here boy!

The canary flutters down. Andra slumps against the bar to avoid it.

NESBITT. (*To Andra.*) It's awright, he was just being friendly! (*To audience.*) See, I telt yi, yi get some right mad bastards in Govan, dn't yi? 'Mon, Shep! Here boy!

He walks the canary out of the door on a lead.

SCENE 9. St Enoch Centre. Outside. Day.
Jamesie and Tracey McGurn are dining in one of the terrace restaurants. A waitress passes. Jamesie hails her.

JAMESIE. (*Showing off to Tracey.*) 'Scuse me. Garçon! I'm afraid this is corked.

WAITRESS. Corked? But it can't be.

JAMESIE. How no?

WAITRESS. It's a cannelloni.

Two people at the next table snigger.

JAMESIE. Look, I don't care if it's a canna export, just get it oot my face afore I wreck the joint, okay?

WAITRESS. Very well.

TRACEY. I love the smooth way you handle these situations, Jamesie. I suppose yi must've got loads of practice when yi were a roadie for Prince.

JAMESIE. Aye, me and the wee man go way back. I knew him

when he was only a viscount. And that's what I was wanting to talk to yi about, Tracey.

WAITRESS. (*Proffering a bowl.*) Cheesey dip?

JAMESIE. Usually. (*Referring to Tracey.*) But she's had a bath today.

(*To Tracey.*) See Princey wants me to go to America and live. So's I can set up his next tour, know?

TRACEY. I see. Could yi not commute?

JAMESIE. I thought about that. Unfortunately thur not enough zones on my travel card.

VOICE. (*Offering.*) Sausage on a stick?

JAMESIE. (*Without looking.*) No thanks.

MCGURN. (*For it is he.*) It's not a choice pal, it's a promise.

Jamesie looks up. McGurn removes his waitress cap.

...Bimbo!

Bimbo sits on his motor-cycle beside McGurn.

BIMBO. Aye Da?

MCGURN. Fast food!

BIMBO. Right Da!

Bimbo revs his motor-cycle. Jamesie realises there's a rope around him.

The bike drives off.

Jamesie's chair is ripped from its table. The bike, the chair and Jamesie go zooming through the Centre.

TRACEY. (*Holding up napkin and pen.*) Gonny get iz Sheena Easton's autograph?

A fading yell from Jamesie.

SCENE 10. Nesbitts' living room. Day.
Meanwhile.

Nesbitt is sitting, watching telly, something about violence, with the canary. Mary is washing the windows. Gash and Burney are sitting. Burney is rocking to and fro compulsively.

BURNEY. Hey Maw.

MARY. What?

BURNEY. See my Da. Has he always been a nutter or is it something he's had to work at?

MARY. Don't you be so lippy.

BURNEY. I'm allowed to be lippy. I'm disturbed.

GASH. (*About Burney.*) Aye. There's his City and Guilds on the wall.

MARY. That's not a City and Guilds, that's a psychologist's report. Rab, will you speak to them.

NESBITT. Look youse, thur nae glamour in violence. Any half wit can go oot and get his self arrested for bodily assault.

MARY. (*To Nesbitt.*) You should know. You've been lifted eighty-three times for it.

NESBITT. That's not the point. The point is, as yi get older yi learn to question things. There's always a reason for violence. It's just a matter of being astute enough to use the old grey matter, know?

He taps his temple. A brick crashes through the window, whapping him on the head. He falls with a grunt.

BURNEY. (*Regarding Nesbitt, to Gash.*) His mooth's a waste of good arse really, in't it?

MARY. (*Stooping, slapping Nesbitt.*) Rab! Are yi awright, Rab!

GASH. (*Finding note attached to brick.*) Hey look, thur a note attached.

BURNEY. What's it say?

GASH. (*Reads.*) 'There is no reason for this. We just like chucking bricks through windows. Sincerely, The McGurns.'

NESBITT. (*Coming to, to audience.*) I don't half talk some amount of shite, don't I?

A shout from without. We hear too the rev of a motor-bike.

SHOUT. Rab! Rab!

NESBITT. (*Hurrying to window.*) Jamesie!

SCENE 11. Street outside the Nesbitts' house. Day.
Nesbitt sees Jamesie on the restaurant seat, lashed to the bike, being dragged down the street.

JAMESIE. (*Shouts, fading.*) Rab! Help me! I'm a take – away!

SCENE 12. Top of high building. Day.
We see Jamesie. We don't see where he is yet. We just hear McGurn talking to him. We observe that Jamesie is in a sitting position.

MCGURN. (*Who is out of view.*) Yi quite comfortable there, pal?

JAMESIE. Fine thanks. I aye prefer a table by the windae.

MCGURN. Don't get lippy.

McGurn gives Jamesie's chair a shake. Jamesie yells, terrified.

JAMESIE. (*Yelling.*) Raaaaaaaaaab!

Our view is extended to reveal Jamesie, suspended on the edge of a very high building, still lashed to his chair. McGurn stands by him, sword in hand.

MCGURN. (*Yelling, waving sword.*) Alfresco ya bass!

SCENE 13. Foot of high building. Day.
A police inspector and a white-coated psychologist are talking. Police cars, policemen are in attendance.

The street is cordoned off. Rednecks are gawping from behind the tape. An ice cream van is doing business.

Nesbitt in attendance, he speaks to audience.

NESBITT. (*To audience.*) Look at them all, eh? It's amazing what comes scuttling oot from under rocks when a wee bit of human drama's on tap. All the social anthropologists and the press and the rubbernecks. In actual fact we're all bigger bliddy cannibals than that eejit is, know what I mean?

Nesbitt approaches a white-coated psychologist and a police inspector.

... Awright boss?

PSYCHOLOGIST. Ah, there you are Nesbitt. Now remember, McGurn is criminally insane. He's pathologically disturbed and socially alienated. There isn't a decent human being alive who could hope to strike up a rapport with him.

INSPECTOR. (*To Nesbitt.*) That's why we're asking you. Will you go up there and talk to him?

NESBITT. (*To inspector.*) No bother boss. (*To audience.*) Amazing what yi get roped into when they offer to waive yir outstanding fines, in't it. (*Passes the canary to the psychologist.*) Here, mind my dug.

(*Spotting Ella.*) Ella hen, yi awright?

ELLA. Bearing up.

A policeman hands her a megaphone.

POLICEMAN. (*Handing megaphone.*) Now remember Mrs Cotter. Your husband's in a state of extreme trauma here. Reassurance is the name of the game, alright?

ELLA. Right.

(*She calls through the megaphone.*) Haw Cotter! Ya knackered white-shoed mobile gland that yi are! You better hope that flesh eating article makes a clean job of you, coz if he disnae I'll be up there to make sure yi make a decent-sized pulp on this pavement!

(*To policeman, handing back the megaphone.*) Thanks, I feel much more reassured now.

SCENE 14. Top of high building. Day.
Meanwhile.

Nesbitt is with McGurn on top of the building. Bimbo is in attendance. Jamesie's still perched on the edge, still in his chair. McGurn is calmer now.

NESBITT. (*Holding a white flag to McGurn.*) Awright?

MCGURN. Awright. (*He pauses.*) You mental?

NESBITT. Do my best. You?

MCGURN. Psychotic with cannibalistic tendencies. (*He smiles.*) That kinna gies me seniority, eh?

NESBITT. I suppose so.

JAMESIE. (*From the edge, his back to the others.*) Rab! It's good to see yi! Well, hear yi anyway!

MCGURN. (*To Jamesie.*) Shut it you! You podgered my daughter!

NESBITT. Ach come on, so did half of Govan. Pamp them all in chairs and yi'd have more seats oot here than the Odeon in Renfield Street.

BIMBO. Hey, that's my sister you're talking aboot.

NESBITT. (*Quieter, to Bimbo.*) Aye, and from what I hear you'd be in the front stalls.

Guilty look from Bimbo. We hear a policeman's voice through a megaphone.

POLICEMAN. McGurn! Come down! Or you're a dead man!

MCGURN. (*To Nesbitt, with an ironic tone.*) Surprise, surprise. Does he not know I've been deid for twenty year. Hey Rab, as one walking time warp to another. Can yi keep a secret?

NESBITT. What's that?

McGurn opens his mouth, puts his fingers in, fishes out a set of false teeth.

NESBITT. (*To audience.*) In the name . . .! Imagine the humiliation. A cannibal with false teeth. (*To McGurn.*) Yir secret's safe with me, big man.

POLICEMAN. (*Through megaphone.*) McGurn, come down!

MCGURN. (*Shouts back.*) Awright, I'm coming, I'm coming! (*To Bimbo.*) Right, Bimbo son, remember what I telt yi. Yi sell the story of yir childhood on a first rights basis only. Separate contracts for overseas TV rights and film options. Full fees up front for all exclusives. Don't do more than three *Wogans* in a single tax year. Cheerio son.

BIMBO. (*Bereftly.*) Da!

MCGURN. Don't you worry son. Oor family's gonny be somebodys as soon as my arse hits the pavement. Oh, and if they go for a mini-series stick out for Gary Oldman. Tony Hopkins is subtle, but he lacks empathy. Be good. (*He calls down to policemen.*) Right ya bams, you asked for it!

He jumps, sword in hand, from the top of the building. Screams are heard from below. Nesbitt peers over the parapet.

NESBITT. (*To audience.*) Not a bad haul eh? One Polis Inspector, two social workers and a psychologist. (*Realisation dawns.*) A psych—! Shep...!

SCENE 15. The park, beside the pond. Day.

Nesbitt, Dodie, Andra and Jamesie are standing near the pond.

NESBITT. (*To audience.*) See when yi get right down to it. Life's like a party. If yi want to make a good impression, yiv got to know the right time to leave, know? Seen this? (*He indicates.*) Govan state funeral.

We see a procession of serious looking people walking behind a battered car as it moves slowly along.

...Pack of wild dogs, black shell suits and a knackered Cavalier.

ANDRA. (*Passing can to Nesbitt.*) Not half a lot of mourners, eh Rab?

NESBITT. Mourners? They're debt collectors. This is the first time they've been able to pin the bastard doon in the one place.

DODIE. Whit'd yeez reckon boys? Can the Crisis Loan Arms do better than that?

ALL. (*Except Nesbitt.*) Bliddy right!

JAMESIE. Rab, I have prepared a funeral for a Govan canary.

He passes Nesbitt a lighted taper.

NESBITT. (*Emotional.*) Thanks, Jamesie. Thanks very much.

We see a funeral boat in the pond, at the edge. It's a beer can with a section cut out and a matchbox opened out and used as a sail.

Nesbitt looks sadly from face to face. He applies the lighted taper to the sail and flicks the boat out to 'sea', reminiscent of a Viking funeral. As he does so we hear the swelling chorus of surging choral vocal.

We watch in close up as tiny flaming match spears sizzle out around and on top of the vessel.

Suddenly a large brick sinks the can with a 'plop'.

Gash and Burney are seen standing by the edge of the pond, throwing stones.

BURNEY. (*To Gash.*) It's the way he would've wanted it.

NESBITT. (*Shouting from some distance.*) Hey! Ya durty little toe rag that yi are...!

A chase ensues. The four men pursuing Gash and Burney.

Domestic

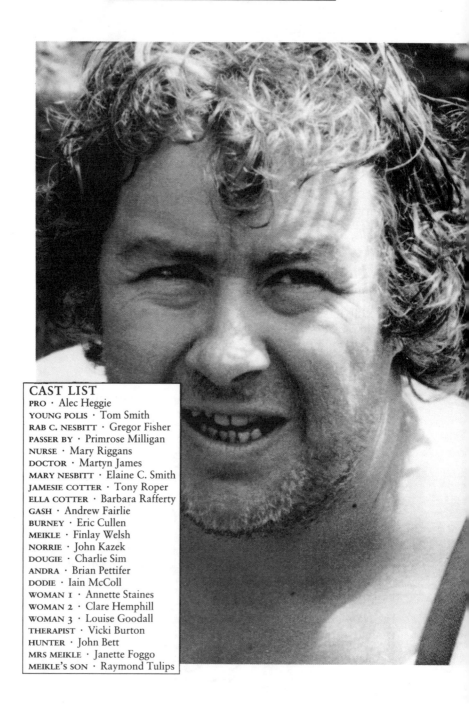

CAST LIST

PRO · Alec Heggie
YOUNG POLIS · Tom Smith
RAB C. NESBITT · Gregor Fisher
PASSER BY · Primrose Milligan
NURSE · Mary Riggans
DOCTOR · Martyn James
MARY NESBITT · Elaine C. Smith
JAMESIE COTTER · Tony Roper
ELLA COTTER · Barbara Rafferty
GASH · Andrew Fairlie
BURNEY · Eric Cullen
MEIKLE · Finlay Welsh
NORRIE · John Kazek
DOUGIE · Charlie Sim
ANDRA · Brian Pettifer
DODIE · Iain McColl
WOMAN 1 · Annette Staines
WOMAN 2 · Clare Hemphill
WOMAN 3 · Louise Goodall
THERAPIST · Vicki Burton
HUNTER · John Bett
MRS MEIKLE · Janette Foggo
MEIKLE'S SON · Raymond Tulips

SCENE 1. Crisis Loan Estate. Evening.

Crisis Loan Estate. Two policemen walking along the street. One's a seasoned old pro. The other's a young rookie.

PRO. Yes, I've seen it all kid. I've stomped around this manor for eighteen years. There's not much I miss on the Crisis Loan Estate. I started here in seventy-five, tell a lie it was seventy-four. Aye changed days.

Nesbitt staggers towards the young policeman, mouth agape, eyes wide. He grasps the young policeman's tunic and slides down it.

NESBITT. *(Sliding down.)* Help me! Help ... me!

He falls, unconscious, to the ground, a knife sticking out of his back.

PRO. *(Still spouting, oblivious to Nesbitt.)* Yes, believe me, yi develop an instinct for trouble ...

YOUNG POLIS. My God! There's a man been stabbed between the shoulder blades!

PRO. Where?

YOUNG POLIS. Here! Right here!

PRO. *(Nonchalantly.)* Oh aye. *(Glancing at Nesbitt.)* What kind of knife?

YOUNG POLIS. *(Looking.)* A bread knife.

PRO. In that case, ignore it. Take a tip kid, never get involved in a domestic. *(They move on.)* I remember a case back in seventy-six. The Crown versus two grannies and a shotgun.

NESBITT. *(Calls.)* Haw!

The policemen stop, and turn.

NESBITT. Look, I don't want to gie yeez compassion fatigue nor nuhing, but d'yi think yi could maybe phone an ambulance, ya bastards that yeez are!

PRO. *(Shouting authoritatively to Nesbitt.)* You looking for trouble, pal?

NESBITT. *(Sarcastically.)* Surprisingly enough I'm not. In actual fact I'm looking for a blood transfusion. Yi huvnie seen one lying aboot the streets by any chance?

YOUNG POLIS. (*Taking pro's lead.*) Go on, on yir way. We don't get involved in domestics.

NESBITT. It didnae take long for you to lose yir idealism, did it? Pretty soon yi'll be a seasoned professional policeman, and be as big a turd as this fat article here.

PRO. Normally you'd pay for that remark. But I don't want yi coagulating all ower my Doc Martens.

YOUNG POLIS. Look, I'll radio in and try and raise an ambulance for yi. Though they're not too keen on venturing into this estate.

NESBITT. Oh very sorry. Next time my wife lunges at me with the breid knife, I'll tell her to hold on while we take a taxi oot to Kelvinside eh?

YOUNG POLIS. Look, do you want me to help or don't you?

NESBITT. (*Struggling to his feet.*) Nah, don't you bother yir archibald. I will stagger alone, boy! I don't bliddy well need yeez, there y'are. Coz I will tell you this, there more than one bliddy knife in my back, there y'are.

(*To audience.*) Don't know why I'm bothering, subtlety's wasted on these people, know what I mean?

The policemen shrug at each other and walk on.

Nesbitt accosts a middle-aged, respectable looking passer by.

... Hey doll, I'm bleeding to death, yi got ten pence till I phone an amblince?

PASSER BY. (*Defensively.*) How do I know yi won't spend it on drink?

NESBITT. Coz if I do, it'll come spurting back oot the bayonet wound in my back. (*He forces coin into her hand.*) Look, here twenty pence for you. Get BUPA to unpucker yir mooth for yi. It's like a sphincter in January! (*To audience.*) Honest to God, if yi want anything done do it yirself.

He staggers on alone.

SCENE 2. Hospital Out-Patients Dept. Late evening.

Nesbitt enters hospital out-patients department. Various people are sitting waiting. Nesbitt approaches the reception desk.

NESBITT. (*To a nurse standing behind the desk.*) 'Scuse me doll, I've had another wee tiff with the wife. And she's went and knifed me between the shooder blades, know! Wacky funster that she is!

NURSE. (*Haughtily.*) Look would yi mind waiting please.

NESBITT. Whit'd yi mean? Whit'd yi mean?

NURSE. Well there's a lot of people here with worse injuries than you, you know.

NESBITT. (*Sarcastically.*) Aye, right enough. I'm a bit of a hypochondriac, know? Whit'd yi mean, worse than mine? (*Turns around to show her the knife in his back.*) Look at that! Look at it! (*Scornfully.*) Worse than mines! I stopped to light a fag in the corridor and the bastards were using it as a coathook!

NURSE. I told you, the doctor's dressing another patient, you'll have to wait.

NESBITT. Bugger that! I'm not gonny be the first patient in here to die of patience! Oot my road!

Nesbitt storms towards the dressing station.

NURSE. You can't go in there! The doctor's giving stitches!

Nesbitt flings open the door of the dressing station.

SCENE 3. Dressing station. Same moment.

A doctor is attending a patient in the dressing station, who happens to be Mary Nesbitt. Mary is having a stitch applied to her finger.

The door flies open. Nesbitt storms in, sees Mary and stands, taken aback.

The doctor and Mary don't notice who is there at first.

DOCTOR. Is that painful, Mrs Nesbitt?

MARY. Not too bad, doctor.

DOCTOR. That nasty knife gave you a troublesome nick but you'll be as good as new in no time.

MARY. (*Enjoying the mollycoddling.*) Thanks very much, Doctor.

NESBITT. (*Propping himself against cabinet. Interrupts.*) Well I'm helluva relieved aboot that I must say. (*To Mary.*) What happened darling? Did yi jar yir pinky when the cold steel juddered against my backbone, was that it?

MARY. (*Noticing Nesbitt. Sulkily.*) I'm not speaking to you. Doctor, tell him I'm not speaking to him.

DOCTOR. (*Reprimandingly.*) The way you treat your wife, Nesbitt, I'm surprised she didn't do it years ago. (*Indicating.*) Lie face down on the couch over there. (*Calls.*) Nurse!

NESBITT. It's nice yir not taking sides nor nuhing. What've I to lie on the couch for? Yir not planning to pull that nasty bread knife oot that troublesome nick in my right lung, are yi?

DOCTOR. Of course. Why not?

NESBITT. Why not? I'll tell you yi why not. That bitch put it there, she can bliddy well pull it oot, there y'are.

MARY. I'm not touching it. You bliddy asked for it pal, don't kid yirsel!

DOCTOR. (*Reaching for knife in Nesbitt's back.*) Don't be ridiculous! You could die, man!

NESBITT. Get yir bliddy paws aff that chib! This is a point of principle here. I'd sooner die than gie into that bitch, there y'are!

MARY. That suits me fine, fella. Coz I'll be straight up that Libra Singles Club while you're still lying in the morgue with a cork up yir arse, there y'are!

NESBITT. Oh I see, it's like that is it? It's like that! Well I'll just live then, I'll live, just to spite yi, there y'are! (*To doctor.*) What you gawping at, get that utensil oot my meat pronto! And make sure thur plenty of blood! (*Pointing at Mary.*) You're in for one helluva washing this Monday, mark my words!

The doctor pulls the knife out of Nesbitt's back, blood spurts.

NESBITT. (*Clenching fist, at Mary.*) Yeeess!

The door opens, Jamesie staggers in, supported by a nurse.

JAMESIE. Awright, Rab?

NESBITT. Jamesie, what happened?

JAMESIE. Ach, Ella stabbed me. She discovered I'd been up the Singles Club.

NESBITT. How'd she find that oot?

JAMESIE. Coz she was there too, Rab. (*Calling behind him.*) In't that right, Ella hen?

ELLA. (*Following behind, skites him.*) Shuttit you! And let me get a look at that jacket. (*Inspects damage to Jamesie's jacket where knife is in back.*) What'd yi think, Mary?

MARY. (*Also inspecting.*) Oh, you've made a rerr job of that, Ella, so yi have.

ELLA. Aye. (*Indicating.*) I always try to stab him doon the seam. It makes the mending easier.

MARY. Aye.

DOCTOR. (*Shaking his head, pouring himself a drink with trembling hand, mutters.*) Domestics!

SCENE 4. The Nesbitts' living room. Day.
There is a fraught atmosphere. Mary is sitting, looking po-faced. Gash and Burney are destroying a chair. Mary draws on a cigarette, anxiously.

GASH. (*To Mary.*) Well, what yi gonny do aboot it?

MARY. Do about what?

BURNEY. Us! We're disturbed! (*Flicking his penis.*) Look, I twiddle my dinger and everything. I need understanding!

MARY. Pack that in you! You're only acting it, just coz the social worker's here!

We see Meikle, the social worker, on the phone.

BURNEY. (*To Gash.*) Did you hear her there? That was violence of the tongue. (*Touching his temple.*) Ah, my psyche! (*To Gash.*) Quick, write the time and date doon, there might be a court case.

MARY. (*Alarmed.*) Oh my God! Don't say things like that you. (*Indicating to Meikle.*) Who the hell put them onto us anyway?

GASH. The polis. The hospital. Could've been anybody. It's yir ain fault. (*Points at Mary.*)

BURNEY. Aye, (*Indicating to Gash.*) look at these eyes, he's got crazed loner written all over him.

GASH. Aye, in five years I'll have snapped and be picking off pensioners from the roof of Safeways with a hunting rifle!

BURNEY. Brilliant! Can I come with yi!

GASH. (*Skites him with stick.*) You find yir ain hobbies!

BURNEY. Aya! (*Calls to social worker.*) Haw pal, I've got another atrocity for yi! Armchair abuse! He's whapping me on the napper with the leg off a Parker Knoll!

GASH. (*Launching the chair at Burney.*) Shuttit you!

BURNEY. (*Launching display cabinet back at Gash.*) Come ahead well!

They launch at each other and writhe on the floor, screaming. Blood flies.

MARY. (*Trying to separate them.*) Pack that in youse! Do yeez want to end up in a home? What's the social worker gonny think?

Meanwhile the social worker has put down the phone. He now stands over Mary. Looming, menacingly. Mary is fearful but tries to make light of the situation.

MARY. (*Wiping some blood from her face.*) Children eh? They can be a handful. (*Proffering plate.*) Another chocolate hobnob Mr Meikle?

MEIKLE. No thank you. Sit down, Mrs Nesbitt. (*Adjusting his wire rim specs, minutely.*) The committee has come to a decision.

SCENE 5. Two Ways pub. Day.
Dodie, Andra, Nesbitt sit, at the bar. Norrie, the new barman, is serving up three pints.

NORRIE. Three seventy-five. (*Nesbitt tosses down money and*

Norrie picks up money from bar.) Here, Nesbitt. What's this I hear about your marriage being on the rocks?

NESBITT. (*Shrugs, he's drunk*.) So, it's a marriage in't it? It's bound to be on the rocks. Do you have a problem with that?

NORRIE. (*Taken aback*.) No, no.

DOUGIE. (*Appearing on the scene. To Norrie*.) True love Govan style, you'll learn.

ANDRA. (*To Dodie*.) Allow the big man eh? Yi know, there are times in my life when I feel like the worst wee numpty jobby in the world. Then I take a swatch at Big Rab there and suddenly I'm walking on air, know what I mean?

DODIE. Aye, yi canny take it away from him. Rab's the loser's loser.

They both look at Nesbitt. He looks back at them, glaring through one eye.

NESBITT. Whit youse looking at? Aye, I know what yeez are thinking. How can one man have so much charisma. (*Turning*

All right, children, you can keep him as a pet. But first we'll have to register him at the post office.

away.) 'Scuse me, while I boak into this ice bucket.

He's turned to heave into the ice bucket. But it has just been removed by Jamesie who is now spooning ice into his drink.

JAMESIE. 'Scuse me Rab. Me and Ella need a few rocks for wur spritzers know?

Nesbitt looks at Jamesie. Jamesie is dressed in relaxed leisure suit and a baseball cap.

NESBITT. Whit yi done up like that for? Is there a sale on at Mothercare?

JAMESIE. Whit'd yi mean? Whit'd yi mean?

NESBITT. The last time I wore claes like that I was in a baby walker with fur balls on my slippers.

JAMESIE. Pack that in! That is typical Govan humour, by the way. The laughter of cruelty. Luckily I've outgrown the need for that. Since me and Ella underwent wur course of empathetic marital therapy.

NESBITT. Therapy? Yi mean yeez've had yir heids looked at?

Ella has joined Jamesie at the bar. She wears a suit that matches Jamesie's. She puts her arm through his.

ELLA. That is correct, Rab. See when that big specialist telt me I was married to a social inadequate with latent deviant tendencies, I felt my heart swell with pride. I'd no idea he was that interesting.

JAMESIE. (*Squeezing her hand, and gazing into her eyes emotionally.*) Ella! (*Turning to Nesbitt.*) Yi should try it yirself Rab. Honest to God, therapy's been the saviour of our relationship.

NESBITT. 'Relationship'? What's with the relationship patter? We're from Govan, man! We don't have relationships, we get merrit! Misery is life's blood to us, it's in the contract. (*Pointing to an old couple.*) Do you, moaning faced bastard take this po-faced bitch for yir wedded wife? Yi do? Well bugger aff and get on with it. I'll see yi in fifty year when I bury yeez!

The old couple, cowering, look at each other.

NESBITT. (*To old couple.*) Nothing personal, playmates, just illustrating a point, know? (*To Jamesie and Ella.*) So bugger off gawn! I was born a cynical bastard. I will die a cynical bastard! And I don't want to sully my lugs with that sentimental treacly keech ever again! Do I make myself clear?

ELLA. It's no wonder your weans hate yi.

Ella and Jamesie turn on their heels and return to their table.

NESBITT. My weans do not hate me! My weans worship the grun I walk on! (*He gets up and totters.*) Stagger on! Even noo they'll be sitting by the fire, in their wee pink pyjamas, waiting for Daddy to come hame. (*Sings, Tom Jones song.*) 'Coz I am coming home to youse ... For I am nuhing without youse...'

SCENE 6. The Nesbitts' living room. Later that day.
Mary is sitting, rocking back and forth, clutching herself with her arms. She is distraught. Nesbitt stands, swaying, a parcel of chips crooked in his arm.

NESBITT. Tain them away? Whit'd yi mean they've tain them away?

MARY. I mean the social worker's putting them into a home, that's what I mean. Do yi want me to spell if out for yi?

NESBITT. I see. And I've brung them back chips tae.

MARY. Oh good! That'll clinch the deal well. (*Calls out.*) Hey pal! Forget the hammerings, the poverty and the emotional bliddy deprivation, my man's brung back chips, we'll all live happily ever after!

NESBITT. Awright, awright. Skip the subtle piss taking will yi! This is a crisis here! I canny believe this! A block just walks into yir hoose then walks back oot again with yir weans under his arm. What the hell kinna society are we running here?

MARY. I don't know what you're moaning aboot. You used to do the same with folks's videos.

NESBITT. That was in the old days. Afore I saw the light. Or should I say afore the light saw me, stepping oot of Rumbelows' window with an Akai up my semmit.

He slumps down into his chair.

I canny take this in here. Yi go oot for a quiet swally, a nuclear parent with two normal, healthy, malajusted weans. Yi come back six hours later yir a childless geek with social leprosy. Yi know, Mary, I'm that upset I can hardly eat my spam fritter.

MARY. (*Exploding.*) I should bliddy well hope not! If yid have been here they might not have taken the weans away! He's been here three times alreadys! Why didn't yi take him seriously!

NESBITT. Coz I'm a cynic, right? I kept waiting for the bottom line. All that talk of warmth and family outings. I thought he was starting off a catalogue with Freemans.

(*Looking at Mary.*) Och, Mary, don't greet!

MARY. (*On the verge of tears.*) What'd yi expect, Rab? They've tain away my boys. I'm at my wits end with worry!

Nesbitt walks over and sits beside Mary.

NESBITT. (*Comforting her.*) Och it'll be awright, hen, you'll see. I'll go alang there first thing the morra afternoon and reason with them. They're bound to see sense.

SCENE 7. Social Services Office. Day.
A chair leg slams down on a desk. A woman is sitting behind the desk, she speaks. Two others sit at desks nearby.

NESBITT. (*Slamming down chair leg.*) Gie me back my weans, ya swines that yeez are!

WOMAN 1. I'm afraid aggressiveness doesn't cut any ice with us, Mr Nesbitt.

NESBITT. No, but a few whaps with this beauty (*Indicating the chair leg.*) might cut a few foreheids though. That's the only way I'm gonny knock any sense into youse people.

WOMAN 2. You see, that's the sort of attitude problem that's got you into this situation in the first place.

NESBITT. I'm not the one with the attitude problem. (*Pointing towards the door.*) Him there! He's the one with the attitude problem!

The social worker has just entered. He stands in the doorway, behind the wall of desks, clutching a folder.

WOMAN 3. (*To Nesbitt.*) Mr Meikle is one of our most respected field officers.

NESBITT. (*Turning to her.*) Oh is that a fact. Well that disnae say hellish much for the rest of yeez. (*Mimics.*) 'O look, there's a dod of scum with a heid bandage and a bottle of Buckfast, he's bound to be abusing his weans, let's run them in.'

MEIKLE. Now, Mr Nesbitt, no-one has accused you of any such thing.

NESBITT. No, but you'll still be peering up their khybers with a Davy lamp just in case, wuln't yeez, aye!

Meikle and his colleagues look at each other, furtively.

And that's what gets me aboot youse people. It's the implicit assumptions. Attitude is it? (*Mimicking.*) 'Oh look, Damien, here's a tight knit community of under-educated social class fives, have a swatch at the manual, see what it says aboot in-breeding. I mean, whit do youse take us for – the British monarchy?

WOMAN 1. Alright, Mr Nesbitt, you've made your point. But you still can't deny that you are of a violent disposition. And that you and your wife are not well balanced parents.

NESBITT. Well balanced? Of course we're well balanced! I'm emotionally deranged and so is she.

MEIKLE. Look, Mr Nesbitt. (*Tapping a wallet file.*) I have a file here full of times, dates, and numerous occasions on which, by the testimony of your two sons, you have struck and emotionally abused them. I'm afraid that until you and your wife learn to change your attitudes your chances of getting your children back are remote in the extreme.

NESBITT. I see, I see. It's like that is it, it's like that? And how the hell are we gonny change wur attitude at oor age?

WOMAN 3. (*To Nesbitt.*) Have you ever tried therapy?

Nesbitt glowers.

SCENE 8. Therapist's office. Day.

Nesbitt and Mary are sitting in a therapist's office. The therapist is making a note on a pad. Nesbitt and Mary are looking anxious and awkward.

MARY. D'yi think this'll work, Rab?

NESBITT. What, us? Turn normal? It's Lourdes yi need to go to for thae kinna miracles, know?

THERAPIST. (*Stops writing. Calls.*) Mrs Nesbitt.

NESBITT. (*To Mary.*) Gawn, doll, pamp yir arse on the couch.

MARY. (*Rising.*) Coming, doctor.

NESBITT. (*To audience.*) I'm pure mortified being here, know? I wish I'd something less socially embarrassing. Like syphilis, maybes. (*Looking over at Mary.*) Talking of which.

We see Mary. She's lying on the couch, with her legs in the air.

THERAPIST. (*To Mary.*) What are you doing?

MARY. Waiting for the stirrups.

THERAPIST. No, no. This is an examination of your psychology, Mrs Nesbitt.

MARY. (*Sitting up.*) Oh sorry, force of habit!

NESBITT. (*To audience.*) That should tell her all she needs to know about her psychology, know what I mean?

THERAPIST. Turning to you, Mr Nesbitt.

NESBITT. Whit aboot me?

THERAPIST. I'd like to ask you about your childhood first of all. Were you close to your father?

NESBITT. Not if I could help it, no. Or I'd get a boot aboot the melt.

THERAPIST. Really. What is your earliest memory of him?

NESBITT. When I was fifteen. I remember the friction burns he left on the carpet when I handed him my first wage packet.

MARY. (*Interjecting.*) Oh my! Well that just shows yi, din't it, doctor? Yi can live with somebody all yir life and yet never really know them.

NESBITT. (*To Mary.*) How, did you no' know my faither was an alkie?

MARY. Aye. But I never knew you had a job.

NESBITT. (*Mutters.*) Bitch!

SCENE 9. Principal's office – children's home. Day.
Scene opens in the principal's office. He's not there, Gash and Burney are there alone. Gash has his feet on the desk, Burney is going through the desk drawers. He swipes some cigarettes from a case on the desk top.

BURNEY. This is the gemme, in't it, being abused!

GASH. (*Swigging from a can.*) Aye, I've not had this much attention since they removed my tapeworm.

A door slams.

BURNEY. Shush! Here the gaffer, act martyred!

The principal, Mr Hunter, enters. Gash and Burney assume submissive poses.

HUNTER. (*Taking his seat.*) Sorry to have kept you. I was just welcoming our new warden, Mr Jethro.

GASH. What happened to the old one?

HUNTER. I sacked him. He was weak on corrective punishment. He lacked . . . imagination.

Hunter twitches compulsively. Gash and Burney glance at each other.

Now, you were saying that your mother is neglectful. That she starved you of love, am I right?

BURNEY. (*As Gash holds him.*) And not only love. She had me when she was past thirty. Her tits had drooped that much I've a hunch in my back through trying to get a breast feed off her. (*His lip trembles.*)

GASH. (*Consoling him.*) There, there.

HUNTER. Well in here you'll have no such worries. We value discipline beyond love.

GASH. (*With a perky smile.*) So you're gonny punish us by pamping us in the kitchens to scrub the dishes, eh?

HUNTER. Dishes? What dishes? You're problem children. Mr Jethro has some very novel ideas concerning intravenous feeding. (*Twitches.*)

BURNEY. (*To Gash.*) Not exactly 'Dunroamin' is it?

SCENE 10. Two Ways pub. Evening.
Andra, Dodie and Jamesie are at the bar. Norrie is leaning over, talking to them quietly.

Mary and Nesbitt are at a corner table, alone, glancing about like threatened animals. Mary is fidgeting. People go to and fro, glancing at them.

NESBITT. For God's sake, Mary, sit still wid yi!

MARY. I canny sit still. I keep thinking they're all talking about us.

NESBITT. Och, they're not talking aboot us. It's just yir imagination. Don't get paranoid, Mary!

At the bar they all turn, as one, and wave, 'casually'.

NESBITT. (*Seeing them.*) Bastards! Whit the hell they saying aboot us?

He moves to go for them.

MARY. (*Restraining him.*) Easy, Rab! Don't get paranoid, remember?

NESBITT. Aye, awright, awright. I'm relaxed. I'm relaxed.

He crosses over to the bar.

DODIE. Evening Rab.

NESBITT. Evening.

JAMESIE. Weans awright, Rab?

Nesbitt leaps instantly on Jamesie, grabbing him by the lapels.

NESBITT. (*Grabbing.*) Whit yi mean by that! Whit'd yi mean by that!

JAMESIE. Nuhing! Nuhing at all!

The others separate them.

. . . Big maniac!

NORRIE. Aye, steady the buffs, Nesbitt. We know you're going through a bad time but there's no need to be so touchy.

ANDRA. Aye, we're yi mates. We've known each other since we were in short troosers!

Nesbitt shoots Andra a look.

. . . Sorry Rab, sorry.

DODIE. (*To Nesbitt.*) Aye, yi can depend on us. We're right behind yi.

He also gets flashing look from Nesbitt.

In a manner of speaking, that is.

NESBITT. Awright. I admit I'm touchy. Of course I'm touchy. Think I don't know thur a whispering campaign going on roon here? Think we don't know they're saying unspeakable things aboot us? I'll tell yi this. It's at times like these yi fun oot who yir friends are, believe me!

JAMESIE. (*Emotional.*) Put it there, Rab. You'll see this through. We have every faith in your innocence!

NESBITT. (*Also emotional.*) Thanks, Jamesie. I appreciate that. That means a helluva lot to me, so it does. (*To Mary, who's now beside him.*) 'Mon, Mary doll. (*To all.*) G'night.

ALL. G'night Rab, Mary.

Nesbitt and Mary go. Jamesie turns to the assembled company.

DODIE. It's a pure shame, in't it. Rab looks that lost.

JAMESIE. Aye. He'll not know what to do with himself with no weans to podger.

Nesbitt's hands clamp on his shoulders.

JAMESIE. (*Disappearing towards the floor, being throttled.*) It was a joke, Rab! A joke!

SCENE 11. Children's home – corridor. Night.
Gash and Burney standing, in a corridor, shivering, in their underwear.

GASH. Sod this!

BURNEY. Well don't blame me. It was your idea to phone the welfare. You said if we got put in a home there'd be vandalism, dangrous drugs and violence!

GASH. Awright, so I'm an idealist. I thought it would be a good place to meet burds.

BURNEY. (*Indicating.*) Err wan err, look.

A girl is being escorted up the corridor. She's in a nightdress with a strait jacket on top. She's muddy, apparently having tried to sneak out.

She's also unconscious. Two attendants hold her upright.

BURNEY. (*To attendants.*) Haw pal, what's up with her?

1ST ATTENDANT. She tried to break out and she's had to be sedated.

BURNEY. I see. Gonny wake her up well, I want to ask her oot.

1ST ATTENDANT. Get tae!

The attendants hurry the girl up the corridor. Hunter, the principal, opens a door behind Gash and Burney and looms out.

HUNTER. (*To Gash and Burney.*) So, Mr Jethro tells me you two have been causing some difficulties. Well we have ways of dealing with troublemakers.

GASH. Aw naw! Are yi gonny pamp us in solitary?

HUNTER. Exactly.

He motions them into a room.

SCENE 12. Inside a bare room. Night.

The same moment. Hunter throws the door wide open. Gash and Burney enter. Inside the room, Hunter turns on a light. Gash and Burney look in, taken aback. We don't see why yet.

GASH. (*Amazed.*) This is solitary?

HUNTER. Well it is till we sort out our overcrowding problem.

We see a roomful of other boys, all in their underwear, in the bare room, shivering.

BURNEY. (*Shivering, to Gash.*) Cheer up. Maybe it's an Anne Summers party.

Ironic look from Gash.

SCENE 13. Social Services Office.

The desks as before. The door behind them, leading to Meikle's office. This time it is closed.

Nesbitt and Mary burst in.

WOMAN 1. Ah, Mr Nesbitt.

NESBITT. (*Slamming his fist on her desk.*) Don't you 'Ah Mr Nesbitt' me!

MARY. Or me!

NESBITT. Wheesht, Mary, I'll do the screaming. (*To woman 1.*) See youse people, yeez sit there with yir fat arses jammed against the radiator, poking yir bureaucratic wallapur into other folks's business! Weans is it? Care is it? Where were youse when she was nursing them through the colic?

MARY. Aye! (*To Nesbitt.*) Come to think of it, where were *you* when I was nursing them through the colic?

NESBITT. For God's sake, can yi not see I'm trying to work up a heid of steam here?

MARY. Sorry Rab.

NESBITT. (*To women behind desks.*) Coz I will tell youse this, thae weans are the fruit of my loins. Awright, fair enough, my loins might be minging and the fruit a bit bruised aboot the extremities, but I brought thae boys into this world.

I'm not violent, I'm misunderstood! What am I, ya toerag?

Mary clears her throat, meaningfully.

Awright, awright *we* brought them into this world! We gied them life! We gied them love! We gied them sixty sodding pence each from the bliddy tooth fairy!

MARY. Which you stole from under their pillows.

NESBITT. 'At's not the point! Thur a principle at stake here! Thae weans is oors! And we are not leaving this office till we get them back!

WOMAN 2. Oh well, no problem.

NESBITT. Whit'd yi mean? Whit'd yi mean?

WOMAN 2. You can have your children back anytime! Elspeth, for God's sake bring them in!

Woman 3 opens the door to Meikle's office. Gash and Burney enter.

BURNEY. Hi Da.

GASH. Hi Maw.

MARY. Oh Son!

Mary hugs Gash.

NESBITT. (*To woman 1.*) Haw, what's the score here, what's gawn on?

WOMAN 1. Mr Meikle sends his apologies. He'd applied for a care order on the basis of what your sons had told him. However, they've since come to us to admit that their evidence has been somewhat 'exaggerated'. Consequently we have little option but to return your children to you with our regrets.

NESBITT. Oh 'with your regrets'. That makes it awright well, din't it eh? (*Slamming fist on desk.*) And where is Meikle? He's put us through hell! How comes he couldnie even gie us these regrets in person?

WOMAN 2. (*Interjecting.*) He can't I'm afraid.

NESBITT. (*To woman 2.*) How no? How no?

WOMAN 1. (*Answering.*) Because he's at home attending a birthday party for his son.

NESBITT. Oh that's bliddy good, that is! Well, far be it from me to keep a father away from his weans!

WOMAN 2. But we warn you Mr Nesbitt. Any further violence against your children and we may be forced to take action again.

NESBITT. Oh, thur's no need for that! (*Throwing his arms round Gash and Burney.*) I'm only too delighted to see my boys! (*He glances upwards.*) Hey look, is that a flying care order?

WOMEN 1, 2 AND 3. (*Turning to look.*) Where?

NESBITT. (*Points upwards.*) There!

While they look Nesbitt bounces Gash and Burney's heads together with a clunk. The women look back.

NESBITT. (*To the women.*) Well thanks for all you've done for us. I don't know what we'd have done withoot yeez! (*To audience.*) Increased wur life span probably. (*To Gash and Burney.*) 'Mon, youse!

Gash and Burney walk, reeling, to the door. Nesbitt and Mary follow them. The three women look at each other, puzzled.

SCENE 14. Garden of Meikle's suburban house. Day.
We get a close up of Nesbitt. We don't see where he is yet.

NESBITT. (*To audience.*) See when yi get right down to it, that's one of the wee lessons in life. Everything has its sequel. I mean, if yi just wait long enough, sooner or later yi get yir chance for revenge, know? (*To someone by him.*) In't that right, pal?

We see that Nesbitt is in the garden of Meikle's suburban house. A children's party is in progress. Some kids sit at a table, gorging themselves. There's a barbecue, a big creamy cake on the table. A banner proclaims 'HAPPY BIRTHDAY LEWIS'.

Meikle is sitting with his wife at the head of the table. Nesbitt is standing over him holding the chair leg from before.

Nesbitt has given Meikle a little nudge as he addressed him. Meikle's wife is nursing her wrath.

MRS MEIKLE. (*To Meikle.*) Are you just going to sit there? That pig has just gatecrashed your son's birthday party. Why don't you hit him!

MEIKLE. You know my philosophy, Amanda. I always reason before I hit.

NESBITT. And I'll tell yi another reason he didnae hit, doll. Coz there's a puddle under his chair! (*There is.*)

MRS MEIKLE. (*To Meikle.*) You were always a wet wick!

Mrs Meikle wallops Mr Meikle in the face and a marital mêlée breaks out.

NESBITT. (*To audience.*) Awright, so maybes it wisnae his fault. But who said life was fair?

Nesbitt is aware of a prod at his side. He looks down. Meikle's son, who looks like a miniature version of his father, is jabbing Nesbitt with a fork.

SON. (*To Nesbitt.*) Look at the mayhem you have caused, you buffoon! Will you please get out of here!

NESBITT. And you can shut yir yap an' all.

He shoves the son's head into the birthday cake.

SCENE 15. Street beside Meikle's house. Day.
At that moment, in the street by Meikle's house, the two policemen from scene 1 are walking past.

PRO. Nah, take it from me, kid. I've been there, done it, seen it all.

YOUNG POLIS. (*Noticing something.*) Hey, look.

They see Meikle and his wife spilling out from the garden, rolling on the ground, lashing at each other with kitchen implements.

YOUNG POLIS. (*To pro.*) Looks like another domestic, John. Whit'd yi think, should we turn a blind eye?

PRO. Nah, son, they're from the professional classes. That would make it a crime of passion. Better book them, 'mon!

The two policemen launch themselves in among the fighting Meikles. Nesbitt stands idly by, watching.

NESBITT. (*In a mock Kelvinside accent, loudly.*) My, would you look at that, Officer. This area's fair gone down. It's no place to bring up children, is it?

MEIKLE. (*Shouts at Nesbitt.*) Bugger off!

NESBITT. (*To audience, innocently.*) His words, not mine!

He places a finger over his lips and continues on his way, mock offended.

Lesson

CAST LIST

DODIE · Iain McColl
ANDRA · Brian Pettifer
JAMESIE COTTER · Tony Roper
RAB C. NESBITT · Gregor Fisher
NORRIE · John Kazek
MARY NESBITT · Elaine C. Smith
BURNEY · Eric Cullen
GASH · Andrew Fairlie
ELLA COTTER · Barbara Rafferty
TEACHER · James Cosmo
ISOBEL/RENA · Susan Nisbet
ISA · Wilma Duncan

SCENE 1. Two Ways pub. Day.

Inside the pub Dodie, Andra and Jamesie are standing near the bar. Norrie is standing behind the bar.

DODIE. Three months Andra.

ANDRA. Three months Dodie. A lot can happen to a man in three month.

Jamesie steps up to the bar, he has highlights in his hair.

DODIE. Yi can say that again. One man can lose his liberty. Another man can lose his wife.

JAMESIE. Awright, awright. Maybes I lost a wife. But things even out in life. At least I gained a hairstyle. (*He admires himself in gantry mirror, combing hair.*)

ANDRA. (*To Dodie.*) He's deep.

JAMESIE. And when that door opens any second, I'll have regained something more important than any wumman.

DODIE. (*To Jamesie.*) A bunnet?

JAMESIE. That's negative talk that. I refute that. I'm talking about a friend!

The door opens. Nesbitt enters, carrying a battered suitcase.

Rab! Ya durty big mockit wet brained keechkicker that yi are!

NESBITT. Jamesie! Ya wee heap of rancid pus! (*To audience.*) That's Govan talk for 'Hullo' by the way.

ANDRA. Hey Rab, yi ready for a swally? (*Proffers pint.*)

NESBITT. Aye, well just the one, Andra. I'll need to get back and make the peace with Mary. (*Accepting the pint he takes a swig.*) Gie her the old sweet talk, know?

SCENE 2. Two Ways pub.

A while later. Nesbitt stands at the bar, swaying. Jamesie, Dodie and Andra are there too. Norrie is serving behind the bar.

NESBITT. She's a bitch, Jamesie! A bitch! I bliddy hate her! Three month in the jug I did because of her!

NORRIE. (*Interrupting. Serving a drink.*) Correct me if I'm wrong. But it was you that stuck the heid on the police horse, was it not?

NESBITT. Well it bliddy asked for it, din't it? Standing there whinnying at me in that stuck up Kelvinside accent. And she coulda stopped it all right at the off. All she had to do was empty the contents of her purse straight into my trooser pocket and we'd have said no more aboot it. Wid she see sense?

JAMESIE. Ach, sure they're all the same, Rab. Sure, that's why I chucked Ella.

NORRIE. Call me a pedant, but was it not Ella that chucked you oot?

JAMESIE. Look, she did not chuck me oot. She invited me to leave.

DODIE. (*To Norrie.*) Aye, if you canny see the subtle distinction there, don't expect him to draw pictures! (*To Andra.*) Hey Andra?

ANDRA. What?

DODIE. What is the subtle distinction again?

ANDRA. Don't ask. So how yi getting on on yir jack anyway, Jamesie?

JAMESIE. Best move I ever made my man? Honest to Christ, I've got my name doon for a double hip replacement, know what I'm saying?

Jamesie does some pelvic thrusts. Andra and Dodie are impressed.

ANDRA & DODIE. (*Together.*) Funky!

NESBITT. (*To Jamesie.*) Whit yi doing?

JAMESIE. Leaving yi my card, Rab. Well, it's not actually a card. But I'll biro my address on yir knuckles there. If yi fancy sharing a billet, get in touch. I could use a striking partner, know? Take a few of my chicks off the subs bench, know what I'm saying?

NESBITT. What. Share a gaff with you? (*Studying the address.*) Live in some glorified cupboard in Govanhill?

JAMESIE. It's not a cupboard, it's a studio flat.

NESBITT. Aye, that's correct. And my lavvy's a billiards room. Don't gie's yir patter!

JAMESIE. Suit yirself, Rab. But it's drink, freedom and rampant nookie against premature middle-age. Now if you'll excuse me, there's a rather charming young lady I'd like to dip. *Ciao.*

SCENE 3. The Nesbitts' living room. Day.

Mary and Ella are sitting on the sofa drinking. Burney is dozing in a chair. Mary looks up at a picture of Nesbitt on the wall and screams.

MARY. Bastard!

BURNEY. (*Lying dozing in chair.*) You talking to me? Trying to gie me a complex or something?

MARY. (*To Burney.*) Not you. *Him.*

BURNEY. Oh, that bastard.

MARY. (*Raising finger to him.*) What've I told you about . . .

The door opens. Gash enters.

MARY. (*To Gash.*) Oh it's you. Where the hell've you been? Have you been drinking again!

GASH. Maw, geez a brek. I don't drink. I was up the youth club playing table tennis.

BURNEY. Aye, using yir eyes as ping pong balls.

GASH. (*Turning on him.*) Shuttit you!

MARY. (*To Gash.*) See you. You'll end up a durty no user like yir Da.

ELLA. (*Rising.*) Ach, leave the wean alone Mary. Don't be so bitter and twisted. (*Tugging at Gash.*) C'mere Son. Gie yir auntie Ella a kiss.

BURNEY. (*Pulling away.*) Kiss that when there's dugs in the street?

Gash frees himself from Ella.

ELLA. I think you want to teach yir weans some manners Mary.

MARY. (*Defensively.*) Don't you stand there and insult my weans.

BURNEY. Aye, that's her job.

MARY. (*Skites Burney.*) Shuttit you.

ELLA. I think I better go Mary. Afore I say something I regret.

GASH. (*Tidying himself. To Ella.*) Aye gawn. And take yir poison darts and yir blowpipe with yi.

MARY. (*To Gash, skiting.*) You be quiet. It was you that started all this.

GASH. Aye that's right, blame me. Yi'll blame anybody but yirself.

He storms out of the door.

MARY. Gash!

Ella storms out of another door.

MARY. Ella!

Burney is sneaking a swig from the bottle. Mary skites him.

MARY. (*To Burney.*) Bastard!

SCENE 4. Street/school. Day.
Nesbitt is staggering up a street. There's a school coming into view.

NESBITT. (*To audience.*) It's at times like these yi wonder where it all went wrong. Yi know my trouble – I married the wrong wumman! Merrit the wrong wumman! (*Takes a sip from a can.*) I mean I don't want yeez thinking I'm getting morose here nor nothing – ya bastards. But see if I could just turn back the clock – or in my present condition – if only I could tell the time. Back to the schooldays, eh? Happiest days of yir life, the schooldays! Some amount of shite I talk. Happiest days of yir life if yi were a sado masochist. And if yi were a school teacher in Scotland in the nineteen fifties – yi probably were a bliddy sado masochist!

Nesbitt gazes at the school entrance, dreamily.

Honest sir, I wasn't smiling. I was just trying to crack my impetigo scabs!

SCENE 5. School classroom (the fifties). Day.
Flashback.

School classroom in the fifties.

Jamesie, now a schoolboy, sits at a desk. Nesbitt, also a schoolboy, takes his place at another. Nesbitt slips his can surreptitiously under his desk flap.

A teacher stands, addressing them.

JAMESIE. (*To Nesbitt, whispering.*) Gie's a swally oot the can.

NESBITT. (*Whispering back.*) At playtime.

JAMESIE. 'Mon you, I paid half.

NESBITT. At playtime! Want us to get the belt offa severe Malky there.

TEACHER. Cotter, be quiet. Or it's the belt.

NESBITT. (*To Jamesie.*) See what I mean? He's a man of his word.

TEACHER. (*To Nesbitt.*) What was that?

JAMESIE. He says yir a lousy turd. It wisnae me, Sur, it was him.

NESBITT. (*To Jamesie.*) Bastard!

The teacher slams a belt down hard on Nesbitt's deskl.

TEACHER. (*To class.*) You all know my philosophy. Children should be seen and not heard. (*Focusing on Nesbitt.*) And 'free dinner children' shouldn't even be seen. (*He looks around the class and sees a girl.*) You girl! Clean the board!

The girl clocks Nesbitt. Her name is Isobel Niddrie.

Nesbitt sees her and does a double take.

NESBITT. Jamesie, Jamesie! Who's that?

JAMESIE. Her? That's Isobel Niddrie. Started yesterday. Yi'd have clocked her if yi hadnie been dogging it. How, d'yi fancy her?

NESBITT. (*Feigning scathing distaste.*) Her. She's hacket!

TEACHER. (*Shouts.*) Nesbitt! When you've finished gawping, perhaps you'd favour us with your attention.

NESBITT. Certainly Sur. What can I do for you?

TEACHER. What you can do for me boy is to stop showing off and read. (*Putting Bible into Nesbitt's hand.*) The Beatitudes. Read.

NESBITT. Read, Sur. (*Holding book as if it were a mystery object.*) Which bit Sur?

JAMESIE. (*To Nesbitt.*) Just the words.

NESBITT. Thanks Jamesie, that narrows it doon a bit. Sarky bastard!

The teacher's belt again slams down on Nesbitt's desk top. Everybody jumps.

TEACHER. (*To Nesbitt.*) Be quiet and read!

NESBITT. Bit of a contradiction there, but I'll do my best. (*To Isobel.*) I'm a bit of a character doll, you'll get to know that.

Belt slams down on desk.

NESBITT. (*Reading.*) Blessed are the pure in spirit, for they shall see the Kingdom of God. Blessed are they that hunger and thirst after righteousness, for they shall be called the children of God. Blessed are the meek, for they shall inherit . . . (*Breaking off.*) . . . Aw come on . . . the first two, maybes. But the meek inheriting the earth, geez a brek! What do they get after the earth? A Ford Popular and a three apartment in Castlemilk?

TEACHER. (*Shouting at Nesbitt.*) Out, boy! That's the Bible!

NESBITT. But the Bible's talking keech Sur.

TEACHER. (*Louder.*) Out! Now!

NESBITT. Awright, awright! I'm coming, I'm coming.

He swanks to the front doing a hard man walk of the type beloved of schoolboys everywhere. When he reaches the front he turns to Isobel, and points at her.

NESBITT. (*To Isobel.*) When all this is over, doll, I'm coming back for you!

TEACHER. (*To Nesbitt.*) Hands out.

JAMESIE. (*Shouts.*) Cover yir wrist with yir sleeve, Rab!

24th. July 1962

Self portrait with willie. (The willie's the one on the left.)

NESBITT. Whit for? He canny draw it.

The belt comes down hard on Nesbitt's outstretched hands, the pain of it catches him by surprise, but he tries to retain the hard man façade.

NESBITT. (*In a high-pitched voice.*) See, telt yi.

TEACHER. Again.

He gives Nesbitt another stroke. Nesbitt struggles to control his facial muscles. He flashes a nonchalant grin to Isobel before going to walk away. He's clearly on the verge of tears.

TEACHER. Where are you going boy? Again!

NESBITT. But Sur . . .

TEACHER. Hands out!

He draws the belt for a third stroke. Nesbitt puts his hands out. He receives the third stroke, his body jerking compulsively under the pain.

TEACHER. (*As Nesbitt genuflects.*) Merely looking at you people is an affront to my sensibilities. But I'm paid to teach you and teach you I will. I will teach you respect. I will teach you the most valuable lesson people of your class can learn – keep your heads below the parapet and you won't get hurt. Work hard and some of you may rise to be mediocre. Who knows, maybe one day one or two of you may even find jobs in an office.

JAMESIE. (*Feigning being impressed.*) Oooooooooooooooohhh!

TEACHER. Cotter! Do you want the same!

JAMESIE. No thanks Sur. But thanks for offering Sur.

TEACHER. (*Turning to Nesbitt.*) Nesbitt, stop blubbing and get to the toilet!

NESBITT. I'm not blubbing. (*Comforting hands under oxters.*) And I canny get to the toilet coz I canny open the bliddy doors can I?

My old teacher, Malky 'Legwarmers' Monteith, prepares for another of his incredibly popular improvisational algebra workshops.

JAMESIE. (*To Nesbitt.*) I telt yi to cover yir wrists with yir sleeve, din't I?

NESBITT. Shuttit you! Or I'll gie ye a boot aboot the melt!

JAMESIE. (*Getting up out of his desk.*) Aye, bliddy try it, puffy paws!

Teacher brings down belt on nearby desk.

TEACHER. (*Shouts.*) Silence!

They all freeze, Isobel rises quietly.

TEACHER. And where do you think you're going, girl! Get back to your seat!

She ignores him and walks towards door.

...Get back to your seat! Sit! I've belted girls before now you know!

JAMESIE. (*Under his breath.*) Aye, I'll bet yi have.

Isobel opens the door for Nesbitt. Holds it open, offering him an awkward smile.

Nesbitt clocks the smile and turns to audience.

SCENE 6. Street/school. Day.
Back to the present.

Nesbitt is still standing in front of the school, dreamily, and holding his can.

NESBITT. (*To audience.*) Did yeez see that there? That wee spark-ette of human decency. That wee instinctive Govan scumball gesture. That was wee Issy Niddrie! I always remember her by that. Of course she could be anywhere noo. She could be roon the corner or in bliddy Kuala Lumpur! But wherever she is – may her arse be parked on a velvet cushion!

He raises the can in his hand, crushes it, drops it into the gutter and kicks it down the road.

Wee Isobel, my first love. Wherever she is now, may her arse be parked on a velvet cushion.

SCENE 7. The Nesbitts' living room. Late evening.

Mary is sitting in her living room, fuming. She's in a housecoat. A door slams off stage. She tenses.

The door opens. Nesbitt appears.

NESBITT. Hullo Mary doll!

MARY. What the hell time do you call this? What am I talking aboot – what the hell month do you call this?

NESBITT. There's no need for the satire – I was in jail, right. I admit it.

MARY. (*Rises, reaches for fags.*) That's big of yi.

NESBITT. Don't be like that, Mary doll. (*Attempting a hug.*) C'mere!

MARY. Don't you come near me, Rab Nesbitt. Yi stagger back here after three month in the jug and expect me to welcome yi with open arms?

NESBITT. (*To audience.*) Open legs'd be better after this amount of time.

MARY. What was that?

NESBITT. Never said a word. Come on Mary. Are yi not pleased to see me? Did yi not miss me?

MARY. (*Sarcastically.*) Oh aye. I missed you pal. In fact I'll show you how much I missed you. (*She tugs him about angrily.*) I've missed polishing the table withoot having to chisel barnacles of snot offa the legs! I've missed the whang of your socks catching me at the back of my throat like cheap supermarket voddy! Oh aye, I've missed you pal! No danger!

NESBITT. What's the matter Mary. Is it your time of the month?

MARY. No it is not my time of the month!

NESBITT. Well then there's no excuse for this carry on. Coz I will tell you this lady . . .

MARY. (*Cutting him dead.*) No, Rab! I will tell you this. I might as well give it to you straight. You were a habit with me. A habit I thought I couldnie do withoot. But noo the habit's broke. And I'm not at all sure I want to start it back up again. Do I make myself clear?

NESBITT. Oh I see. You're not sure you want me back. Well I'm not bliddy sure I want to be back! So what'd yi say to that lady?

A suitcase comes hurtling at Nesbitt. He ducks.

MARY. If yi don't like it – sling yir hook. That's what I say to that!

The door opens, Burney enters, rubbing sleep from his eyes.

BURNEY. Hey Maw. Gonny keep the rammy doon. I'm trying to kip.

NESBITT. Burney, Son!

Burney sees Nesbitt.

BURNEY. (*Hiding behind Mary.*) Mammy, Mammy, who's that strange man?

NESBITT. It's me! It's yir Da!

BURNEY. I know it's you, ya tube!

NESBITT. (*Lunging towards him.*) Don't you speak to me like that or I'll...

MARY. (*Wielding a poker*) Try it! And yi'll go oot that door in instalments!

NESBITT. (*Trembling lip.*) Oh I see, it's like that is it? It's like that? Yeez are all turning against me noo!

MARY. I'm not turning against yi. Nobody's turning against yi.

Gash appears from behind Burney and Mary.

GASH. (*To Nesbitt.*) I'm turning against yi. Bugger off!

NESBITT. Right, I bliddy will. (*Picks up case.*) I don't want yeez. I don't bliddy need yeez. I will walk alone, boy! I will walk alone!

SCENE 8. Two Ways pub. Day
Andra, Dodie and Nesbitt are at the bar. Norrie is behind it.

NESBITT. (*Drunk.*) I telt her. I just said 'Right, yir finished! Finito! From now on you are amnesia city!'

DODIE. That's the gemme Rab. It's the only way to treat them.

ANDRA. (*Giving Dodie a sidelong glance.*) Eh?

DODIE. (*To Andra.*) For God's sake humour the poor bastard, his arse is oot the windae.

ANDRA. (*To Nesbitt.*) So whit yi gonny do now, Rab?

NESBITT. What am I gonny do now? I'll tell yi. See that door? See when that door opens, I'll have regained something more important than any wumman, there y'are.

The door opens. Jamesie appears.

JAMESIE. Rab!

NESBITT. Jamesie! Yi got my message?

JAMESIE. I got yir message, Rab. What can I say? You can stay with me anytime!

NESBITT. Thanks, Jamesie, that means a lot to me (*To all.*) Did yeez hear that? That's what yi call friendship. Coz I will tell you this. Yes, I might be keech. Yes, I might owe a stack of dosh on the provvy, but even keech can find its place in the sun!

JAMESIE. (*To all.*) I hope youse are taking notes here. Coz see that man (*Indicating to Nesbitt.*) – he's inspirational. See you Rab. You could be the Winston Churchill of Wine Alley! (*He picks up a pint.*)

NESBITT. Bliddy right, Jamesie. We shall swally on the streets. We shall swally on the beaches.

JAMESIE. We shall swally in the kebab shop and pish up a close later.

NESBITT. We shall never go sober.

JAMESIE. Freedom, here we come!

NESBITT & JAMESIE. (*Together.*) Hulloo!

SCENE 9. Bedsit. Night.
Jamesie's bedsit. The door flies open. Jamesie enters. He mimics a great fanfare and bows, respectfuly. Nesbitt enters, cautiously.

NESBITT. Is this it?

JAMESIE. Certainly this is it. Whit'd yi mean is this it? D'yi not like it?

Nesbitt starts to speak, then gags.

JAMESIE. What's the matter?

NESBITT. Nothing, nothing. Just the smell's kinna catching at my throat, know?

JAMESIE. Oh that? That'll be the air freshener.

NESBITT. You mean there's air in here?

JAMESIE. Don't gimme that. There's plenty of air in here! All the air yi want blowing in through that warp in the windae fitting. Noo c'mere and I'll show yi yir bed. (*He indicates with a flourish to a poky looking bed.* 'Er look! This is yours.

NESBITT. That's my bed?

JAMESIE. Aye. How? What yi looking for?

NESBITT. The Cindy doll that fits it.

JAMESIE. Ach, quit moaning. It's a stoater of a bed. Go on, fling yirself doon. Luxuriate.

Nesbitt sits on it, tentatively, then looks up at Jamesie, twisting his lip.

JAMESIE. Now what is it?

NESBITT. The sheet cracked.

JAMESIE. Aye well. I've been meaning to get doon the laundry. But I'm aye oot with some chick, yi know how it is.

NESBITT. (*Holding up a stiff smelly green length of material, with disgust.*) Is this a towel?

JAMESIE. Look, gonny stop moaning! What's the matter with the towel?

NESBITT. (*Sniffs it, looks at it.*) Nothing. 'Cept if yi dried yirself with it yi'd end up smellier than before yi washed.

JAMESIE. (*Snatching towel away from him.*) That is a slur! If

you're gonny live under my roof the least yi can do is show me some respect. I only took you in here coz I'm a compassionate bastard, a fool to myself.

NESBITT. Ach yir arse! The only reason you want me here is to pay half the rent of this flea pit and coz yir feart to sleep in the dark!

JAMESIE. That is another slur. That's two slurs! Two slurs rapid, I'll not forget this. I feel sullied!

NESBITT. Sullied? Yir bliddy boggin, pal. Look at thae jeans!

JAMESIE. Leave me alane. Women like me like this. It makes me look vulnerable.

NESBITT. Vulnerable? Christ any more vulnerable and yi'd be weaving baskets at Rampton.

JAMESIE. Well if yi don't like it, bugger off!

NESBITT. I canny bugger off noo, can I? I've burnt my bliddy boats noo haven't I. But I will tell you this boy, I'll not be spending any more time in this . . . Kinning Park Hilton than I have to, believe you me! I mean look at the place! Thur not even a honnel for the door!

JAMESIE. Aye there is.

NESBITT. Where is it well?

JAMESIE. (*Pointing.*) That's it propping up the armchair. (*Pause.*) Look I didnae want to have to live here. I didnae want my marriage to break up did I?

NESBITT. I know yi never. I hear what yir saying. (*Pause.*) Look, yi want that cup of tea?

JAMESIE. Aye, get the kettle on.

NESBITT. (*Glancing about.*) Where is the kettle?

JAMESIE. It's in the sink.

NESBITT. (*Looking about again.*) Where's the sink?

I know what you're thinking! 'D for Dunce.' But you're totally wrong! It's D for Dickhead actually.

JAMESIE. It's ahint that curtain in the dine-ette. I've been meaning to get it fixed.

Nesbitt pulls open a curtain.

NESBITT. In the namea God!

We are shown a sink choked with dirty, mould-ridden dishes.

JAMESIE. Quit moaning, I'll clean it up!

NESBITT. Nah, yi'd better leave it. Yi might upset the balance of nature, yi go meddling with that sink. By Christ, Jamesie, look at it. It could be a metaphor for our life. (*Distantly.*) Who'd have thought back in the old days that we'd have ended up like this?

He lapses into a dreamy smiling reverie.

SCENE 10. School classroom. Day.
Flashback to the fifties again.

We're back in the classroom. The teacher is at his desk. Nesbitt stands before him.

TEACHER. (*Looking up.*) So Nesbitt. This is your last day of school.

NESBITT. Yes Sur. Just came to say cheerio, Sur.

TEACHER. Well I can't say I'm sorry to see you go. What are eight tens?

NESBITT. Same as ten eights, Sur.

TEACHER. Same recalcitrant attitude all the way down the line. You've been a waste of space.

NESBITT. Cheers Sur. Just like to say thanks for all the help and encouragement you've given me.

TEACHER. (*Points to another pupil.*) You girl, you're leaving too?

Isobel stands and nodds.

TEACHER. (*To Isobel.*) What are you going to do with your life?

ISOBEL. Raise a family Sir, same as my mother.

TEACHER. (*Curtly.*) Predictable. And you, Nesbitt?

NESBITT. Raise a glass Sur, same as my father.

TEACHER. I've no doubt you'll both achieve your ambitions. Goodbye.

Isobel and Nesbitt turn to go.

TEACHER. (*Calling.*) Nesbitt?

Nesbitt turns back.

NESBITT. Sur?

TEACHER. You'll be dead in a gutter by the time you're forty.

NESBITT. That's a bit uncouth Sur. I mean you're half deid in a semi in Paisley but I don't go ripping the pish out of you. (*To audience.*) That's the middle class all over. No manners.

SCENE 11. Bus stop. Day.
Mary, Gash and Burney are waiting in a queue at the bus stop. It's cold. Mary sees an old friend in the bus queue.

GASH. Bliddy city! Bliddy buses!

MARY. Quiet you. It's cold for all of us.

Mary's friend approaches.

ISA. Hullo, Mary hen.

MARY. Oh hullo Isa, how's it gawn?

ISA. I'm just saying – I'm awfie worried about Ella. She's going right doonhill, so she is.

MARY. Whit'd yi mean?

ISA. (*Spelling out.*) D.R.I.N.K. And she was at the doctors. For P.I.L.L.S.

MARY. (*Clocking Burney listening in and says . . .*) Hey Jodrell Bank, bugger off. (*To Isa.*) Oh my! Poor Ella!

ISA. What about yirself, Mary. Where yi off to?

MARY. Och, well I'm taking this yin (*Indicating to Burney.*) to the correction unit. And that yin into the child psychologist (*Indicating to Gash.*). Kinna Govan equivalent of a family picnic, know?

They notice a man, staggering and singing his head off. It's Nesbitt.

. . . Oh no, there a drunk man. (*To Gash and Burney.*) Don't youse look.

GASH. Oh yir awright Maw. It's not a man. It's my Da.

We see Nesbitt staggering along the road with a fish supper in his hand.

NESBITT. (*To audience.*) Some place the Govan eh? Where else can yi get a fish supper at nine o'clock in the morning? Easy! Just whap it off the drunk that's been lying pished ootside his close all night! (*He sees Mary and the boys and calls.*) Well are yeez gonny say hullo or what?

Burney goes to speak, Mary plants her hand over his mouth.

MARY. (*To Burney.*) Shuttit you. I don't want youse speaking to him.

BURNEY. But he's wur Da. We're entitled to speak to him.

MARY. He's a lousy selfish immature big moothed swine that buggered off and left us in the lurch – but I don't want to poison yir minds against him. Speak to him if yeez want.

GASH. No, Maw's right. He deserves to suffer. Let's gie him the rubber ear.

NESBITT. (*Hearing all of this.*) Oh it's like that is it? It's like that. Well don't think I'm gonny come creeping about, trying to sneak in with yeez. (*To Burney.*) Burney son, want a chip?

BURNEY. Stick yir chips up yir arse.

MARY. (To Burney.) Hey, what've I told you. Manners.

BURNEY. Please.

MARY. That's better. Now let's walk up to the next stop. There's some dodgy looking characters about here.

BURNEY & GASH. Right.

They go.

NESBITT. Well go on! Gawn! (*Flings chips away.*) I will walk alone boy! I will walk alone! (*To audience.*) Yi know my trouble? I married the wrang wumman. I married the wrong bliddy woman! Bastards!

He turns, walks straight into a tree and falls. And we hear the tweet of birdsong as he slips unconsciously into the past.

SCENE 12. Park. Flashback to the fifties. Day.
Nesbitt and Isobel sit under a tree, kissing. Nesbitt, on finishing his kiss, resumes eating a packet of crisps.

They have recently finished school.

NESBITT. What've you got a big reddy for? Was that your first kiss?

Isobel nods.

. . . Good kisser in't I?

Isobel nods again. She spits out a lot of second-hand crisps.

Isobel was a special person and I respect and cherish the memory of our association and hold it in the highest esteem . . . By the way, I shagged her on the first date.

NESBITT. Sorry Isobel. I should've finished my crisps afore I kissed yi.

ISOBEL. It's awright. It's great being on a picnic, sure it is? I've never been on a picnic afore.

NESBITT. Govan picnic. (*Indicates to their picnic.*) Ten fags and a bottle of Tizer.

He puts his hand on her knee. Tries to slide it up her skirt. She stops him.

ISOBEL. You stop that you!

NESBITT. What's the matter, you no' want it? I want it, gonny gie's it? Gonny Isobel, please gonny!

ISOBEL. Yir no' getting it! Whit'd yi take me for? D'yi take me for a slag. (*Nesbitt starts to move.*) Where yi gawn?

NESBITT. I'm just gawn, right? I've been going out with you for ages.

ISOBEL. Three weeks.

NESBITT. Exactly. I mean don't get me wrang. I don't want to pressurise yi nor nothing. I don't want to get tore in with the moral blackmail nor nuhing. But put it this way, if you don't gie me I'm gonny chuck yi.

ISOBEL. Don't.

NESBITT. It's up to you. It's oot of my hons, doll.

ISOBEL. But if I do gie it yi'll chuck me tae.

NESBITT. (*Moving in close.*) Naw, doll, naw. Yiv got it wrong. I'm not like the other blocks, I'm different.

ISOBEL. Yir patter's the same.

NESBITT. Aye, but my feelings are different doll.

ISOBEL. How d'yi not speak yir feelings?

NESBITT. Of course I speak my feelings ... through my hons. (*His hand is on her knee.*) And right now my hons are saying ... gonny drap yir drawers please.

ISOBEL. (*Restraining him.*) Wait! If I do it ... yi better not chuck me. I mean it!

NESBITT. I'll not. Promise. You're precious to me. (*Fumbling with her clothing.*) How does this bra undo?

ISOBEL. (*Restraining him again.*) I mean it! You're precious to me tae. I feel dead protective aboot yi. Yi bring oot my mothering instincts. But I'm warning yi, if yi chuck me I'll get my three cousins to stiffen yi.

NESBITT. (*Steering her.*) Lie down.

ISOBEL. (*Sitting back up.*) Wait! (*She looks about.*)

NESBITT. What is it? Have you done it before?

ISOBEL. (*She shakes her head.*) I always wondered where I'd do it first. That's all I've thought about for ages. That and who I'd do it with. Never thought it would be with you. Here. In the keechy old Elder Park. With the keechy old cranes and the squashed doubts and the dog keech. Probably in the same keechy spot where my faither lay slavvering and grunting on top of my mammy fifteen years ago. (*Pause.*) Y'll have gathered I'm nervous.

NESBITT. (*Comforting her.*) Yir awright. We're not like them. We're different. (*Guiding her away.*) 'Mon into the bushes.

They run a few steps, then stop.

ISOBEL. We are, aren't we? We'll not end up like them, will we?

NESBITT. Geeza brek. Do I look like a loser?

SCENE 13. Jamesie's bedsit. Evening.
Jamesie is in bed with a girl. We can't see her face. We hear Jamesie murmuring to her.

JAMESIE. Oh Rena, Rena, gonny gie's it. Gonny, gonny.

We hear a crackling noise.

RENA. What are you doing? Are you eating a packet of crisps?

JAMESIE. No, I'm taking off my underpants.

RENA. Well yi can just put yir underpants right back on again!

She sits up. We get a good look at her face. She looks extraordinarily like Isobel.

JAMESIE. Awright, awright.

The door opens. Nesbitt enters. He has a cut face.

NESBITT. Jamesie, I'm back.

JAMESIE. Lovely to see yi, Rab. Now gonny pish off, I'm entertaining.

RENA. Not to me yir not. (*To Nesbitt.*) Pleased to meet yi, I'm Rena.

NESBITT. (*Shaking her hand.*) Do I not know you, doll?

JAMESIE. (*To Nesbitt.*) Don't start that patter.

Jamesie puts his arm round Rena.

RENA. Get yir paws aff me, Jamesie!

Jamesie leaps out of bed.

JAMESIE. I don't know what it is with you. You musta got all the respectability chromosomes in your family. Coz yir sister certainly had nane.

NESBITT. Her sister? (*To Rena.*) Who is yir sister, doll? Would I know her?

RENA. Yi might. Isobel Niddrie.

NESBITT. Never! Did yi hear that Jamesie? Wee Issy Niddrie? How's she keeping doll?

JAMESIE. She's deid.

RENA. Died two years ago. Now that's how I don't like him talking about her. (*She skites Jamesie.*) Now you keep yir lip zipped in future!

JAMESIE. Awright, steady the buffs. Goodwill unto stiffs and that.

Jamesie looks over to Nesbitt. He's looking stunned.

JAMESIE. Hey, did I not tell you that Rab? I thought I telt you

We've made life's whacking great cosmic journey together — all the way from school to the social security.

that. A year, two year ago, a block came up to me in a pub, he said, 'Hey guess who's deid? Wee Issy Niddrie.' I says, 'Naw, I must tell Rab that.' And I was gonny and the next thing this other block taps me on the . . .

NESBITT. (*Stops him dead.*) Shuttit, Jamesie! Just shuttit! (*To Rena.*)What happened to her, doll?

RENA. She merrit a bad man. He ran away and left her with two weans to bring up. The strain killed her.

JAMESIE. Snap! Bit like yirself, eh Rab! Small world!

NESBITT. Awright! I don't need semaphore to see the comparison, do I?

JAMESIE. Hey come on, no offence to her memory but a stiff's a stiff! And we're still alive! We ought to enjoy ourselves! Come on, what'd yi say! It's ran dan night! (*He looks at the two long faces. Tries to get them going. Singing, dancing.*) Aa-a-atmosphere! I love a party with a happy atmosphere. And I will take you there, tomorrow we'll be dancing.

Mary enters, Jamesie sees her first.

JAMESIE. Mary!

NESBITT. Mary doll. Thank God!

MARY. Aw, shut it Rab. (*To the dancing Jamesie.*) Haw, Jive Bunny.

JAMESIE. Whut?

MARY. You better get yir arse in gear and get up that Southern General intensive care unit pronto.

JAMESIE. Whit for?

MARY. Ella's took an overdose.

Mary exits. Nesbitt follows, running.

NESBITT. (*Calling after her.*) Mary, Mary, wait for me! Wait!

Jamesie is left, standing. He ponders for an instant, shrugs his shoulders, resumes dancing.

JAMESIE. (*Singing.*) Atmosphere. I love a party. (*To Rena.*) Wives, eh? They'll do anything to spoil yir night.

Rena gives him a solid right hook on the face. Jamesie falls over.

JAMESIE. (*On the floor. Rubbing jaw.*) What was that for? Selfish bitch!

SCENE 14. Street/school. Night.
Later.

Nesbitt is pushing a squeaking, battered pram along the street. It's full of clothes, suitcases, bin liners, junk.

He stops, strikes a match on a lampost, lights up.

NESBITT. (*To audience.*) Helluva life awthegither in't it? I mean if the present disnae get yi, the past jumps up and whaps yi on the napper. I'd four brothers all snuffed it. I survived coz I was the only one that could understand the claim form for Family Credit. Survival of the fattest kinna style, know. Ach but then I shouldnie complain. The nineties suit me in fact. I used to be a drunk, noo I'm a leisure concept. Yi get a lot of leisure concepts in Govan. Big fat bastards in trainers and shell suits stoating aboot with a six pack and a fish supper balanced on their bellies. Ach but still, a toon's what yi make it. Wish to hell they'd make it Monte Carlo, but I suppose we're stuck with it.

He reaches school. He stops briefly. The playground is silent.

...forever onward, eh?

He squeaks onward up the street.

SCENE 15. The Nesbitts' living room. Evening.
Later that evening.

Mary is fussing about, tidying. She's obviously expecting someone.

Gash and Burney are sprawled on the chairs.

MARY. (*Chivvying the boys.*) Come on youse, get hep! Yir da'll be here any minute! This is supposed to be a celebration!

Ella enters from the kitchen carrying a tray of drinks.

ELLA. A double celebration!

MARY. Coz four working class toerags are back thegither again! (*Looking at Ella's tray.*) Is that the celebration toast, Ella?

ELLA. Right here. Thunderbird for us and raspberry cordial for the boys. (*To Burney.*) D'yi like raspberry cordial, son?

BURNEY. I don't know. Pamp a few aspirins in it and I'll tell yi.

ELLA. (*Defensively.*) Are you getting at me? (*To Jamesie who has entered from the kitchen, carrying a plate.*) Is he getting at me?

JAMESIE. No, no, that's just good natured banter Ella. Aimed at taking the sting oot a delicate emotional situation. In actual fact, he's helping you to come to terms with yir trauma. By ripping the pish oot yi. So, eh, fruit cake Ella! (*Proffering plate, sniggering.*).

GASH. (*Holding out a bicycle pump.*) Stomach pump Ella?

MARY. That's enough youse! Pack that in! Ella's been through a bad enough time! She needs our sympathy and support.

ELLA. Don't worry, Mary. I can look after myself.

JAMESIE. Exactly. (*He shivers.*) Turned kinna cauld the night, Ella. D'yi want yir strait jacket on! (*Sniggering.*)

Ella, in a lightning swoop, grabs Jamesie by the balls.

JAMESIE. (*Frantically.*) Ella! Stop! It's not my fault yi tried to top yirself!

ELLA. I did not try to top myself, Jamesie. It was accidental. What was it?

JAMESIE. (*In a high-pitched voice.*) Accidental!

ELLA. Exactly. And if I ever catch you dropping as much as one veiled hint to the contrary (*Giving him a squeeze.*) you better hope there's somebody walking aboot oot there with a bollock donor card! Do I make myself clear?

JAMESIE. (*In agony.*) Very clear Ella.

ELLA. (*Letting go of Jamesie's balls.*) Good.

Jamesie is bent double. Gash proffers him some fruit.

GASH. Grape Jamesie?

Interesting theological dilemma – do I still love my neighbour, even if he's the Antichrist?

JAMESIE. Very bloody funny!

A door slams offstage.

MARY. Wheesht everybody! Here he comes! Noo remember. This is his home. He's entitled to feel he belongs here. And I don't want anybody saying anything to belittle his confidence. Awright?

ALL. Awright.

MARY. I might be keech. But I'm auld-fashioned keech. And when keech marries it marries for life. I want this to work.

The living room door opens. Nesbitt enters, sheepishly.

MARY. Hullo, Rab.

NESBITT. Hullo, Mary doll.

Nesbitt gives her a wee kiss. Mary blushes bashfully.

ELLA. Welcome back Rab.

NESBITT. Helluva nice to be back Ella. (*He sees Jamesie.*) Awright, Jamesie?

JAMESIE. Awright, Rab.

They buddy punch a bit. Nesbitt makes a playful grab for Jamesie's balls. Jamesie jumps back in panic.

JAMESIE. (*With a frantic smile.*) No, Rab, no! (*Making an excuse.*) Yir spilling my drink, big eejit!

NESBITT. Sorry Jamesie. (*He focuses on Gash.*) Nae bother, Gash son, eh?

GASH. Nae bother, Da!

They buddy punch. Nesbitt clocks Burney. He sits, sour faced, on the settee.

Mary and Nesbitt share a look.

NESBITT. Burney son. Daddy's home.

BURNEY. So it is. Never recognised yi there with yir eyes focused.

MARY. (*To Burney.*) Look, what did I tell you!

NESBITT. It's awright Mary doll, I'll handle this. (*Producing something from his pocket.*) Look Burney son, I was just going through some old schmutter the other day when I came across this – it's my old Waverley! I made that in school.

Burney grabs the balsa wood paddle steamer from Nesbitt, looks at it scathingly.

BURNEY. Is that it? I thought at least it would be some back-dated pocket money. Is that the best yi can do in emotional bribery?

NESBITT. (*Taking it back from him.*) Oh, I'm not gonny bribe yi with it, son.

BURNEY. Whit yi gonny do with it well?

NESBITT. I'm gonny ram it right up you...

Burney darts off. Nesbitt pursues him. They zoom out of the door.

Mary and the others watch, and listen.

Off stage, we hear Burney scream.

BURNEY. (*Off stage.*) Ah! Aah! AAAHHHHH!

MARY. (*To all.*) Oh well. Rab's back!

ALL. (*Raising glasses.*) Hull-oo!

Life has Meaning

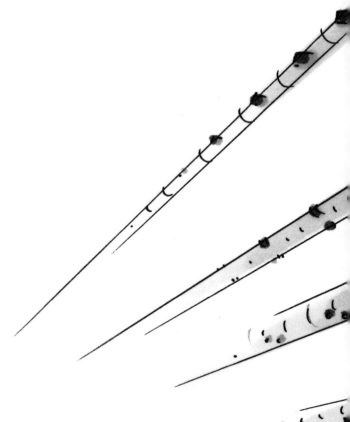

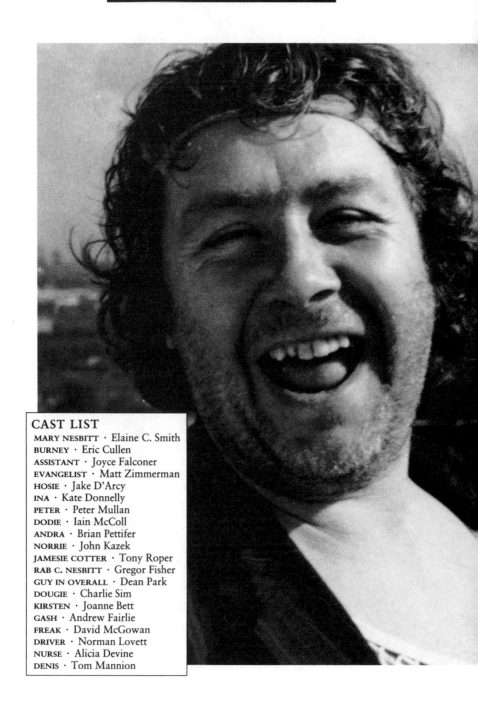

CAST LIST

MARY NESBITT · Elaine C. Smith
BURNEY · Eric Cullen
ASSISTANT · Joyce Falconer
EVANGELIST · Matt Zimmerman
HOSIE · Jake D'Arcy
INA · Kate Donnelly
PETER · Peter Mullan
DODIE · Iain McColl
ANDRA · Brian Pettifer
NORRIE · John Kazek
JAMESIE COTTER · Tony Roper
RAB C. NESBITT · Gregor Fisher
GUY IN OVERALL · Dean Park
DOUGIE · Charlie Sim
KIRSTEN · Joanne Bett
GASH · Andrew Fairlie
FREAK · David McGowan
DRIVER · Norman Lovett
NURSE · Alicia Devine
DENIS · Tom Mannion

SCENE 1. Supermarket. Day.

In the supermarket.

Mary and Burney are standing at the check out, a long queue is behind them. Mary's groceries are being rung through by the assistant.

She's watching them closely with a worried eye.

Burney picks up a packet of sweets. Mary skites him and takes them.

MARY. *(To Burney.)* Put them back! Or you'll not eat yir tea.

BURNEY. Usually they are my tea.

MARY. Wheesht will yi! *(Turns and speaks to the queue.)* Honestly, weans!

Mary turns back, looks into her purse, and bites her lip, as she views the contents.

BURNEY. What's the matter, Maw?

MARY. Govan roulette, son. Buying messages without checking the contents of yir purse first. Still, sometimes in yi life yi need to flirt with danger.

The assistant rings up the last item.

MARY. *(To herself.)* Here we go, apocalypse now.

ASSISTANT. *(To Mary.)* Twenty-eight pound ninety-seven.

MARY. *(Steadying herself.)* In the namea God! *(Composed.)* I wonder if yi could just put a few things back please dear? I'll keep everything with sugar in it, yi can hold onto the rest.

ASSISTANT. *(Snottily.)* I see. *(Removing items.)* Anything else yi'd like me to put back?

MARY. Aye. The clock. To twenty year ago when I could last afford a message bag.

She holds up her grocery bag. It has one handle. It snaps under the weight of the groceries and sugar starts to cascade from a broken bag.

MARY. Jesus wept!

SCENE 2. Peter the warlock's house. Evening.
Outside the front door of another house in the Nesbitt street Hugh Hosie stands at the door, with a carpet runner under his arm. His small van is parked in the street.

A bigger van goes past, from which an American evangelist is spouting his message through a microphone. On the side of the van is a message saying 'Life has meaning'.

EVANGELIST. For the Lord said 'Behold I am the light and the way! Whomsoever believeth in me shall have everlasting life!'

HOSIE. (*Mutters.*) Bams!

The evangelist is heard, fading, as his van moves up the street.

Hosie rings the doorbell.

FEMALE VOICE (INA). (*From inside the house.*) It's open!

Hosie opens the door and enters.

SCENE 3. Peter the warlock's living room. Evening.
Hosie is still standing outside the front door.

We can hear chanting from inside of the house 'We worship thee O Satan...' On the word 'Satan' the door begins to open and Hosie shouts inside...

HOSIE. Missus, I've brung the carpet.

As the door fully opens, the scene inside the living room beyond comes into view. A number of chanters kneeling on the floor in a circle. They are all very ordinary-looking people. But they are all naked.

Hughie stands, watching the scene, shocked.

From behind a curtain we hear noises of passion: 'Ooh, ooooh, oooooohhhhhh...' etc.

The chant continues from the circle in the living room. 'We worship thee o Prince of Darkness.'

The woman of the house, a middle-aged, dowdy-looking soul, looks at Hosie. Her name is Ina.

INA. (*To Hosie.*) Just coming.

The sounds of passion from behind the curtain climax . . . and recede.

INA. (*Shouts towards the curtain.*) Peter!

PETER. (*Shouts from behind curtain.*) Whut is it?

INA. The block's here with the carpet!

PETER. (*Still out of view.*) Right.

Peter emerges from behind the curtain. He is a warlock, as is evidenced by his small distinctive beard and swept back hair. He is also naked. He stands, takes a draw at a cigarette, and looks over to Hosie.

PETER. (*To Hosie.*) The nights are fair drawing in, eh?

HOSIE. (*Still standing stunned at the front door.*) Have yi . . . had yir holidays yet?

PETER. Nah. We thought we'd have the hoose done up instead. That's how we ordered the carpet, know?

HOSIE. Oh aye! Where'd yi want it, by the way?

PETER. Just in the lobby thonder. Ina'll show yi. I've got a goat to sacrifice.

Someone brings Peter a goat on a lead, and hands him an axe.

HOSIE. (*Nervously.*) I see. Right. Nae bother. (*He picks up the carpet.*)

INA. (*To Hosie, indicating to a door.*) Just through here.

They exit from the living room.

HOSIE. (*To chanters as he passes them.*) Nice meeting yeez.

SCENE 4. Lobby of Peter the warlock's house. Evening.
A moment later.

Ina and Hosie are standing in the lobby of same house, the chanting has resumed from within the living room.

INA. (*To Hosie.*) Just here. On the stairs.

HOSIE. (*Kneeling.*) Right y'are.

INA. Sorry about the noise. D'yi worship the devil yirself?

HOSIE. Me? Nah! (*Eager not to offend.*) But I've a mate that's an Ozzy Osborne fan.

INA. Anything I can get yi? A cupp-a tea or that?
HOSIE. No thanks.

An animalistic scream is heard.

INA. Some blood then? It's fresh!

Hosie shakes his head, vigorously.

SCENE 5. Two Ways pub. Day.
Andra, Dodie, Jamesie, Hosie are at the bar. Hosie is telling his tale. Norrie is behind the bar trying to dislodge something from the ceiling with an upturned brush.

DODIE. (*To Hosie.*) Bare?

HOSIE. Naked!

ANDRA. In the raw?

HOSIE. In the raw rumping bare buff wobbling lick tip tickling scuderoony!

NORRIE. Sod it! (*Giving up with brush. Turning his attention back to the bar.*) Anything I can get youse guys?

JAMESIE. (*Physically uncomfortable.*) Start with a Kleenex.

NORRIE. (*To the others*) Bunch of weans. Yir as bad as that bam ower there (*Indicating.*). Stuck a dart in the ceiling last week as a protest against my management. Nothing'll budge it.

At the place Norrie has indicated Nesbitt is sitting alone, arms crossed, looking severe.

NORRIE. (*Calls to Nesbitt.*) Yi awright, diddums, yi got rid of yir petted lip yet?

NESBITT. Don't you speak to me Judas. And I'll not speak to you!

NORRIE. I'm running this pub noo. And I'll do it whatever the hell way I like. In't that right, Dougie?

Dougie, now a customer, is also at the bar.

DOUGIE. Young blood rules Nesbitt! (*To Norrie.*) Gawn yirsel son!

NORRIE & DOUGIE. (*Doing high 5s.*) Yo!

NORRIE. (*To Nesbitt.*) And if I want a virtual reality machine in my pub I'll bliddy well have one.

JAMESIE. (*To Norrie.*) Ach, don't take it personal, Norrie. Rab's just narked coz he's been warned aff the swally. (*He calls to Nesbitt.*) Hey Rab, another fruit juice?

Nesbitt picks up his empty glass, crushes it in his hand.

JAMESIE. (*To Norrie.*) Take that as a no.

ANDRA. A Virtual Reality Machine? Is that what that high tech armchair is ower there?

We see a machine over by the wall. A guy in overalls is putting the final touches to fixing it up.

DODIE. Aye, we thought a disabled guy must've parked it there till he used the lavvy.

NORRIE. Aye, yeez can laugh. But these machines is all the go. They can recreate any human experience, no matter how wild or dangerous.

GUY IN OVERALL. (*Calls over to bar.*) That's it ready. Who's first for blast off?

They all look at each other, tremulous, excited, like kids at a fairground.

NESBITT. (*To audience.*) Look at them. Magic eh? Designed by NASA to train astronauts. Ends up as a toy for dickbrains in a pub in Govan. One small step for man!

ANDRA. (*Shouts, excitedly.*) Me! Me! I'll go first!

They all whoop and cheer. The guy in overalls puts headphones on Andra and sits him at the machine.

ANDRA. (*Sitting down.*) Mister, mister, what experience can I simulate!

GUY IN OVERALL. Whatever you like. (*Proffering control panel.*) Choose a button.

Andra does so, and leans back. The machine starts up. We hear computer-game-type sounds. Andra is freaked.

ANDRA. Oh man! Too much! Too much!

They all watch, intrigued, from the bar.

JAMESIE. (*To Dodie.*) Is that blood coming oot his ears? Magic! (*Calls.*) Hey Rab! You're missing yirself! 'Mere and see this!

NESBITT. (*Crossing over to bar holding stem of glass.*) Aye, I see it. Very good.

ANDRA. My mind! Nnnnngggghhhh! My minddddddddd!

NESBITT. What experience is that he's simulating?

HOSIE. (*Looks at control panel.*) Having a job.

NESBITT. (*He whistles between his teeth.*) Crazy bastard!

JAMESIE. Hey Rab, you want to be next?

NESBITT. Not me boy. There's too much of this escaping from reality nooadays. What would I want to simulate?

HOSIE. Being drunk?

They all snigger. Nesbitt, fuming, plonks his glass stem down on the bar.

NESBITT. (*To Norrie.*) Same again you!

NORRIE. (*Looking at stem.*) Clean glass?

The door opens and Peter the warlock appears wearing a flowing robe.

PETER. (*Calls to Norrie.*) Hey Jim. Awright if I bring my pet in?

NORRIE. If yi keep it on a lead.

HOSIE. (*Excitedly, to others.*) That's him! That's the guy I was telling you aboot! The warlock!

PETER. (*Leading in an alsatian.*) Here, Prince. Heel!

They all clock the dog. It's got a horn, like a unicorn.

NESBITT. (*To Dougie.*) In the namea God horned beasts, loony machines and devil worshippers! D'yi need to be some kind of tweedledum to drink in here?

DOUGIE. Don't knock it. I served you for years.

NORRIE. (*To Peter.*) What can I get yi pal?

PETER. White rum. With black ice.

Slight double take from Norrie.

PETER. (*To Nesbitt, having heard his last comment.*) You got a problem pal? (*Looking about.*) Anybody here got a problem with satanic worship?

Everyone is uneasy.

JAMESIE. Satan? No! Great wee devil, eh boys?

HOSIE. Aye. Bit of a rogue but loveable with it!

ALL. Aye.

PETER. Good . . . I mean bad.

NESBITT. (*To Peter.*) Aye, I've got a problem with it.

PETER. What's that?

NESBITT. What gies you the right to throw yir weight aboot in this pub? Yi stoat in here with a dug with a wart in its nut and a swirling cloak that's straight oot of Freemans' catalogue and yi act as if yi own the joint!

PETER. I resent that. This cloak belonged to Aleister Crowley.

NESBITT. Oh aye? What was it, the great beast's duvet cover?

Dodie, Hosie and Jamesie snigger. Peter shoots them a glance. They fall silent, and freeze.

NESBITT. (*Indicating to the others.*) Yi might impress this bunch of rejects from the Twilight Zone but yi don't impress me.

Andra staggers from the machine towards them.

ANDRA. (*Rubbing his eyes.*) Holy keech, what a trip. It's good to get back to Govan. (*He sees Peter with the dog.*) What the hell am I simulating now?

JAMESIE. Normality.

ANDRA. (*Shudders.*) No chance! (*To Norrie.*) Pint of Thunderbird and an aspirin tops! (*To Jamesie.*) Joke's a joke, know?

PETER. (*To Nesbitt.*) Yi know your trouble my man, you huvnie learned respect for the ancient wisdoms. As a result I'm afraid I'm gonny have to curse yi. (*He clicks his fingers.*) There yir cursed.

NESBITT. Was that it? Was that the curse?

PETER. A right good cursing. Take it from me, you will meet with an accident very soon and die a horrible excruciating death. Nothing personal. (*Drains his glass.*) Noo, if yeez'll excuse me I've a unicorn to sacrifice and a virgin to deflower. See yeez.

He turns to go.

DODIE. He must be a warlock right enough, to've fun a unicorn in Govan.

JAMESIE. Never mind that. He must be a Sherlock Holmes to've fun a virgin.

HOSIE. You not worried Rab?

NESBITT. Worried? What, because some deranged numptie with an over-active trooser wand is trying to put the whammy on me? Listen, it'll take a bit more than a few shirt pins stuck in a Cindy doll to worry me!

The door opens, Peter looks in, he clicks his fingers. The dart drops from the ceiling into Nesbitt's head.

JAMESIE. See you Rab. Yir uncanny. Really got yir finger on the pulse.

NESBITT. (*Very distressed.*) NNNNNNNNNNNNNN!

JAMESIE. (*Wrestling with dart in Nesbitt's head.*) Hold still.

Nesbitt yells.

SCENE 6. Two Ways pub. Day.
Meanwhile.

Peter exits the pub with dog. Burney is about to enter. Paper bag slung over his shoulder. As they pass each other.

Okay, so he drinks blood, deflowers virgins and runs a coven but that doesn't make yi a bad person, does it?

BURNEY. (*To Peter.*) Hey Jim, want a paper?

Peter ignores him, walks on with dog.

(*Calls.*) ... What about yir wife?

Peter turns, Burney's already ducked into the pub.

SCENE 7. Two Ways pub. Day.
As before.

Jamesie is still wrestling with the dart. Nesbitt is yelling.

Burney stands in the doorway.

BURNEY. (*Calls to all in the pub.*) Erzi late night fin-el! (*Calls.*) Hey Da, want a paper?

NORRIE. Yir faither's got a dart stuck in his heid son.

BURNEY. (*Noticing the situation.*) So he has. Whit kinnda score d'yi get for that Da?

NESBITT. Bugger off! Little swine that yi are! (*Lashes out at Burney.*)

We view the door. Gash and his girlfriend Kirsten enter. They are carrying leaflets.

KIRSTEN. (*To Gash.*) That evangelist is inspirational. He just makes yi feel like spreading the Lord's word, doesn't he Gash?

GASH. Aye right. But do we need to spread it in here?

NESBITT. (*Pain, as dart is pulled out.*) Jesus wept!

KIRSTEN. (*On hearing this. To Gash.*) Perhaps you're right. We'll convert the lounge bar instead.

They turn to go. Nesbitt calls.

NESBITT. Gash son! Yi awright?

KIRSTEN. Do you know that person, Gash?

GASH. Oh, only very vaguely. He's something to do with my mother's children. The father or something.

KIRSTEN. (*Confused.*) I see.

BURNEY. (*To Kirsten.*) Hey doll, want to buy a paper?

Kirsten turns, Burney clocks her.

... Oh it's you. I thought there was a draught in here.

GASH. (*To Burney.*) Pack that in you. Kirsten's a very warm person.

BURNEY. (*To Gash.*) Yir arse (*To Nesbitt.*) Hey Da, did yi hear that yin?

NESBITT. (*To Gash.*) Aye, nae offence son. I'm not saying she's cold nor nuhing. But every time she opens her mooth a light comes on.

KIRSTEN. (*To Gash.*) I'm going. Give me a call in a couple of millennia when you and your family have evolved!

She storms off.

GASH. (*Calling after her.*) Kirst! Kirst!

NESBITT. Don't blaspheme, son. Yi might gie the lassie a bad impression.

Nesbitt and Burney laugh.

SCENE 8. The Nesbitts' living room. Day.
The family are sitting separately. Nesbitt is in his chair, regarding the others.

Burney twirls the corner of a hankie into a point and sticks it up his nose.

Mary sits chewing her lower lip, anxiously, the contents of her purse spread on her lap. She's counting it out.

Gash is sitting, rocking to and fro in a foetal crouch.

NESBITT. (*To audience, quietly.*) What's it all about, eh? Life Has Meaning. Except for viewers in Scotland, of course. (*Regarding the family.*) Who are these people? How'd I come to be with them? (*Regarding Burney.*) See that effort? I hate that wee article with every fibre of my being. Know how? He reminds me too much of myself.

MARY. (*Absently.*) Did yi do much today, Rab?

NESBITT. Aye. I got cursed by a warlock. I'm gonny die a horrible and excruciating death.

MARY. (*Not taking it in.*) That's good. It's nice to have a hobby.

NESBITT. (*To audience.*) Deaf bitch. All the same she's been a good wife to me. See that wumman? See if it came to a choice between wee Michelle Pfeiffer or that wumman? I'd choose Michelle Pfeiffer. But at least I'd have the decency to feel guilty aboot it, know? That's the kinna big hearted bastard I am.

We see Gash rocking back and forth by the fireplace.

NESBITT. (*Looking at Gash. To the audience.*) By Christ, look at that fizzer, eh? Like an A to Z of the human psyche. Seventeen year old and he's so anally retentive he's still shiteing rusks. The human frame bared to the nerve. But underneath it all ... underneath it all ... the notion of some infinitely gentle, infinitely suffering thing.

GASH. (*Looking at Nesbitt.*) Whit you gawping at ya ugly big bastard!

NESBITT. (*To Gash.*) Don't you speak to me like that, I'll pamp my fist doon yir pulmonary tract!

MARY. (*Still counting, angst ridden.*) Oh shuttit youse! I'm trying to tally up!

GASH. I will not shuttit! It's his fault my burd chucked me!

BURNEY. (*To Gash.*) Don't talk mince!

GASH. Whit'd yi mean?

BURNEY. Thur's not a burd in Govan that husnie got calluses on her elbows from giving you the nudge.

GASH. Kirsten wasn't like that. She was religious.

NESBITT. Whit difference did that make? She sung a hymn while she booted yir arse out the cowp. (*Making blessing motions.*) 'Gettest thou to fu ...'

GASH. (*Launching himself at Nesbitt.*) Foul mouthed swine that yi are! I've had enough!

Gash attempts to throttle Nesbitt.

NESBITT. (*Fighting him off.*) Get aff! Get tae! Traitorous wee swine that yi are!

BURNEY. (*Incensed.*) Hull-oo!

He pees on the electric fire, causing it to spark and crackle, wildly.

MARY. (*Locked in her own private torment.*) I must go on. I can't go on. I'll go on. Och sod it, will I buggery!

She upsets the coins from her lap, heads for the window, throws it open and climbs out.

SCENE 9. Street/window ledge. Day.
At the same moment.

The evangelist is passing in his van. We see the 'Life has meaning' slogan on the side of the van.

Mary is on the window ledge. She's tottering, on the brink of jumping off.

She hears evangelist spouting his message.

He looks up, seeing Mary on the ledge.

EVANGELIST. (*Through the microphone to Mary.*) Reject despair! For make no mistake, she that will open her heart to the word of the Lord will feel the healing balm of his loving and almighty embrace!

Mary bites her lip. She looks back into the living room.

SCENE 10. The Nesbitts' living room. Day.
At the same moment.

The living room from Mary's point of view. She is still on the window ledge. Gash is at the door, screaming at Nesbitt.

Nesbitt's got a saucepan on his head, blood trickles from his temple. (Gash has obviously chibbed him.)

Burney is ripping huge chunks of paper from the walls.

NESBITT. (*To Gash.*) I don't want you back in this hoose again, boy!

GASH. Don't bliddy worry! I'm offski! I'm gawn away to find myself!

NESBITT. Well beat it! Afore yi find yirself on the end of my boot!

He removes the saucepan from his head and chucks it at Gash, who scarpers.

... Ya prodigal wee bastard that yi are!

SCENE 11. Street/window ledge. Day.
Meanwhile.

Mary is on the ledge as before. She's seen the scene in the living room, now she turns back to look at the evangelist.

MARY. (*To evangelist.*) 'Scuse me, yi know how yeez say that 'Life Has Meaning'? Is that even for people with Provident lines?

EVANGELIST. (*Calling back to her.*) Yes, even for people with Provident lines.

MARY. (*To audience.*) It's as well to ask. Afore I go making an arse of myself walloping tambourines.

SCENE 12. Two Ways pub. Day.
Andra, Jamesie, Dodie and Nesbitt are at the bar. Nesbitt is drunk. Norrie is serving.

NESBITT. I mean religion! I ask yi! Two thoosand bliddy year it's been here and it's still not worked! I mean why don't we at least privatise the Archbishop of Canterbury or somehin? Maybes make some dosh on a share issue oot the auld swine. Recoup some of wur spiritual losses sorta style, know?

NORRIE. I liked you better when yi were teetotal, Nesbitt. And I didn't even like you then.

NESBITT. Ach unpucker yir face, sanctimonious swine. See that yin, he's a Christian in reverse. Turns his wine into watter!

Restrained chortling from all.

JAMESIE. You want to watch yirself, Rab. That's heretic talk. The God fella's chibbed folk for less than that.

NESBITT. That a fact. Well the God fella'll need to get in the queue, boy. My arse is promised to the Antichrist, remember?

DODIE. (*To Andra.*) Allow the big man, some nerve, eh?

NORRIE. (*Proffering coin.*) Did you want change for the virtual reality machine, Dodie?

DODIE. The machine? Sod that. I'll just watch big Rab's pupils dilate instead.

We see Nesbitt's eyes. They're wild, rolling.

DODIE. (*He shudders, to Norrie.*) Noo that's what I call a walk on the wild side. (*He takes a stiff drink.*)

JAMESIE. He shouldnie drink. He's been off it too long. (*Taking Nesbitt's arm.*) 'Mere Rab.

NESBITT. Get tae! Get thee behind me Cotter! (*To Norrie.*) And you get thee in front of me a pint of Mick Jagger pronto! Religion is it? Don't talk to me! It's ruined my bliddy life boy, there y'are!

JAMESIE. How'd yi mean Rab?

The door opens and Mary enters, rattling a tin.

MARY. (*To a stranger.*) 'Scuse me, can I ask yi to spare a few coins please?

Nesbitt, recognising the voice, spits out his drink.

ANDRA. Mary doll. Whit yi doing in here?

MARY. Collecting for the underprivileged. (*Oozing.*) Many are so grateful, you know.

NESBITT. (*To Mary.*) Bliddy right they are! Bliddy right! I'm underprivileged but I don't see yi rattling a tin on my behalf!

MARY. You? I widnae rattle a stick in a shit pail for you, pal.

Someone drops a coin into her tin. She's immediately oozy again.

MARY. Bless you. (*Pinning a flag on them.*) Many thanks.

NESBITT. (*To Mary.*) Bliddy good in't it! Talk aboot bliddy hypocrisy! That's what gets me aboot youse people! With one face it's (*Mimicking.*) 'Bless you, many thanks' and with the other it's 'oh it's you, get yir erse oot my coupon'. Yi make me bliddy sick, ya multi faced oozy unctuous bitch that yi are!

MARY. Don't you speak to me like that. Religion's changed my life!

NESBITT. Aye, and I'll change yir bliddy features if I get any mair of yir patter, gawn, get oot my sight.

He goes to take a sip of his pint. A familiar voice speaks.

GASH. (*For it is he. To Nesbitt.*) Like a flower for the lady?

We see Gash. His head is shaved. He has a ponytail and is wearing a robe.

MARY. Gash, whit the hell have yi done to yirself, son?

GASH. My name's not Gash noo. It's Delicate Child of the Eternal Moon.

NESBITT. (*To Gash.*) Whit yi gibbering aboot?

GASH. I've joined a rare religious sect. We believe in the innate harmony of the universe. So I've changed my swining name to Delicate Child of the Eternal sodding Moon! Noo do yi want to buy a bliddy floower or don't yi!

NESBITT. Aye, as a matter of fact I will. I'll buy the whole bunch of them!

GASH. Good. It's aboot time you treated my maw better.

NESBITT. (*Taking the bunch.*) Oh I'm not treating yir maw son. These are for you.

He snatches Mary's collection box from her and places it into Gash's hands.

...Here! (*Turning the flower stems upwards.*) I'm gonny stuff these doon your delicate bliddy karma hole! (*Attempts to ram them down Gash's throat.*).

GASH. Aya!

MARY. (*Leaping onto Nesbitt's back.*) Get aff him! Leave that bliddy wean alane!

ANDRA. (*To Jamesie.*) Religion's really changed the Nesbitts hasn't it?

JAMESIE. (*Looking at the Nesbitts.*) Aye. They're more at one with each other.

We see and hear the tangle of arms, legs, fists, cursing, swearing, fighting, rolling on the floor, with Norrie trying vainly to separate them.

SCENE 13. Two Ways pub. Day.
Seconds later.

At the pub doorway. Norrie is ejecting Nesbitt.

NORRIE. Gawn, get oot and don't come back! (*He goes back inside and slams the door.*)

NESBITT. (*Shouting back at shut door.*) I'll not bliddy be back, don't you worry! I hope yir tongue cleaves to the roof of yir dental plate! And may there be a plague of locusts in yir beer cellar! But they'll have to drive oot the bar flies first! Toerag!

He turns, fuming. A Jesus freak stands in front of him, with some leaflets.

FREAK. (*Proffering one.*) Leaflet, sir?

Two potent arguments against banning vivisection on dumb animals.

NESBITT. (*Curtly, with restraint.*) No thank you.

FREAK. (*Smugly.*) It wouldn't harm you to take one.

NESBITT. And it widnae harm you to take one of these. (*He nuts him.*) When I say no, I mean no.

The freak falls to the ground

(*Shouting down at him.*) Yi think yiv got a bliddy monopoly on God just coz yiv turned religious. God's word is it? If I was God, I'd be more fussy who I had spreading my word. Cos I widnae hire you to spread marmite on my toast, boy!

At that moment Peter happens to pass with his dog.

PETER. (*To Nesbitt.*) Oh it's you. You not deid yet? That curse shoulda worked by noo.

NESBITT. Don't you bliddy start, ya feeble minded fourth division Faust that yi are! Yi think yir bliddy malevolent coz yiv got a gonk roon yir neck and a dug with a cornetto on its napper!

He pulls the 'cornetto', then let's it go. It's on elastic so the dog howls painfully.

There is no devil boy! Satan does not exist!

PETER. Pack that in you, that's blasphemy!

NESBITT. Well if he does bliddy well exist why doesn't he strike me doon noo eh? (*Shouts.*) Come on ya durty big horny swine that yi are, do yir worst! (*Nothing happens. Nesbitt takes a couple of steps.*) Yi see, it's nuhing but a load of bliddy . . .

Suddenly Nesbitt is hit by a van, hard. We hear the evangelist's voice say . . .

EVANGELIST. For Jesus said 'I am the light and the way'.

Nesbitt looks up from the ground. We see the 'Life has meaning' van. The evangelist peers over at Nesbitt, looking concerned. The driver speaks.

DRIVER (COLIN). (*To Nesbitt.*) You alright?

NESBITT. (*Looking up, bloodied and dazed. To audience.*) That's a turn up for the book, in't it?

At which point Burney appears, carrying his newspaper bag. He leans over Nesbitt.

BURNEY. (*Proffering a newspaper.*) Hey Da. *War Cry?*

Nesbitt's hands come up, reaching for Burney's neck.

SCENE 14. Hospital ward. Evening.
Nesbitt is in a hospital bed on a drip feed. Someone next to him is on a life-support system.

NESBITT. (*To audience.*) Helluva life awthegither, in't it? Yi sit aboot, scratching yir arse for forty year then in the space of a day yi get cursed by the devil, denounced as a heretic then some happy bastard runs a truck ower yir heid to show how at one with mankind he is. But see when yi get right down to it, it's birth, copulation and death. The rest is guess work. Look at this. (*Indicates person next to him on life-support machine.*) This is what we talk aboot when we talk aboot life. There's not a peep oot him, thur a funnel up his arse and a breeze between his ears but what the hell, his guess is still as good as oors.

We see a steady blip on the monitor screen.

... (*To audience.*) All he knows is – shut up and keep gawn! And I for one canny make any philosophical advance on that, can you?

A nurse arrives, with a hypodermic in her hand.

NURSE. Here you are, Mr Nesbitt. Just a little jab. It'll take away the pain.

NESBITT. (*To the nurse.*) Take away the pain eh? Allow it! I coulda done with one of these when I was paying my last phone bill, eh hen? 'Make someone happy with a phone call' (*The nurse jabs him.*) And yi know who the 'someone' is, don't yi? It's the greedy bastard that keeps jacking up the bliddy charges! (*To nurse.*) Just a wee bit of banter hen. To put yi at yir ease. Coz I warn yi, yi'll be here all night. Jabs don't take with me, I've got this abnormally high resistance know?

He slumps back, out cold. His eyes are open, but he's not at home. His limbs are like lead. He's only dimly aware. Speech is a great effort.

NESBITT. (*Very slowly.*) See ... telt ... yi.

The nurse looks up, the evangelist has entered.

EVANGELIST. Mr Nesbitt, nurse?

NURSE. Ah, Mr Maharg. I'm afraid I've just put him out.

EVANGELIST. Well perhaps I could just sit by him and offer a short prayer?

NURSE. Well I really shouldn't. He is in Intensive Care. But I don't suppose it'll do any harm.

EVANGELIST. It might even do some good.

NURSE. (*Going.*) Quite.

The evangelist kneels by Nesbitt. Nesbitt's eyes see him, but he can't speak.

EVANGELIST. (*To Nesbitt.*) I know you can't speak, so don't even try. But I come with a message of hope.

NESBITT. (*Slurring, totally inaudibly.*) Get ... to ...

EVANGELIST. We've come together as a result of an accident. An accident that has left you in some degree of physical pain.

NESBITT. (*Slurring.*) Bliddy ... right ... boy.

EVANGELIST. But you know, in a strange way, there's no such thing as an accident. Each occurrence, however irrational, is part of the Lord's scheme of things. What we call an accident can be the Lord's way of bringing a man to know his word. So that his spirit may blossom and his life be charged with meaning.

NESBITT. (*Alarmed, eyes widening.*)Nnnnnnnnnnn!

EVANGELIST. So you see, in a strange way, there truly is no such thing as an accident.

The evangelist rises. As he does so his foot pulls a cord, disconnecting the life-support system linked to the guy in the next bed.

EVANGELIST. (*To his driver who has appeared.*) Come Colin, there is more good work to be done.

The evangelist gives the driver a little self-congratulatory hug. They exit.

Nesbitt's eyes register anguish.

We see the monitor, it has stopped blipping. A hand fits the plug back into the wall, we see Gash as he straightens up.

GASH. (*To Nesbitt, slinging a bag down.*) Here ya bam, I brung grapes. (*He mutters after the evangelist.*) ... silly bastard!

The monitor blip starts up again.

NESBITT. (*Noticing the blip. To audience.*) Halle ... fuckin ... lujah!

SCENE 15. The Nesbitts' living room. Day.
It's party time at the Nesbitts, and Andra, Jamesie, Dodie and Nesbitt are drinking. Ella is also in attendance. Nesbitt is in full cry, kneeling before Mary, serenading her.

NESBITT. (*Singing.*) 'Eef I a-had my a-life to a-live overrrrr, I'd a-steeel a-fall in a-love with a-you...!'

He lifts Mary's hand, moves it, picks up a bottle of Thunderbird and kisses it.

... Wacky Rab's back! Wee visual joke there, Mary, know?

MARY. Is that right? Here another yin to keep it company.

She gives him a skite.

NESBITT. (*Rubbing his head.*) You're no fun since yi lost yir faith.

MARY. I didnae lose my faith, I couldnie afford faith.

(*To Ella.*) Three pound seventy-nine for a jar of Nescaff to host the coffee morning, Ella. Christ, I was that desperate I ended up knocking one oot of Safeways. Kinna defeated the moral object, know?

ELLA. Aye, it's a wicked world, Mary. There's too much immorality these days.

Jamesie, Dodie and Andra are at the wall listening to the sounds from Peter the warlock's house next door.

JAMESIE. (*To Ella and Mary.*) Hey, gonny youse rap it? Thur a block in here trying to deflower a virgin!

ANDRA. Aye, have some consideration.

MARY. Rab, you'll need to do something here. These people'll be corrupting our weans!

NESBITT. Ach, not at all. No way. We've brought thae boys up decent! Are you trying to tell me the last fifteen year of parental guidance have been a complete waste of time? Coz if so, my whole life has been in vain!

SCENE 16. Peter the warlock's living room. Day.
Meanwhile.

In the living room of Peter the warlock's house. The same bunch of nudes are assembled. We see that Gash and Burney are amongst them, chanting away.

GASH & BURNEY. (*Together.*) Hail Satan, Prince of Darkness, we adore thee!

BURNEY. (*From side of mouth, to Gash.*) Haw! Where's the virgin they're sacrificing?

GASH. (*Sidelong, indicates.*) Ower there.

We see that he is indicating to an ugly girl.

BURNEY. Yir kidding. I thought that was the goat.

...a appears, she holds up her hand.

.... Hail Satan!

... Hail Satan!

... Hail Peter, Prince of Darkness.

... ail Peter, Prince of Darkness!

...pears.

... ank you. Well I must say it's encouraging to see so many
... ucifer in tonight. Because you know, evil has been
... of a bad name lately. Frankly, devil worship has been
... ed by the gutter press. Sure, we sacrifice goats, yes we
... ns and indeed on occasion we do daub our naked
... warm blood of animals and engage in unspeakable
... epravity. But does the public ever read, ladies

and gentlemen, about the wonderful work we do for charity? Hmm?

Applause and whoops from the others.

The doorbell rings.

INA. Erri door, Peter. Will I get it?

PETER. No I'll go. You polish the boning knife.

SCENE 17. Peter the warlock's house. Day.
Outside.

Nesbitt is standing in front of Peter's house.

NESBITT. (*To audience.*) It's queer what yi find yirself having to do these days, in't it? Twenty year ago you might nick next door to ask yir neebor to turn his telly doon. Five year ago it was his ghetto blaster. Now it's to ask him if he widnae mind not usurping the moral order and mindbending yir weans into sucking yir liver oot yir arse through a goat horn. Still, needs must when the devil drives, eh?

The door opens, Peter stands there erect.

NESBITT. (*To Peter.*) Haw. You. Do you renounce the devil and all his works?

PETER. No. How?

NESBITT. Thank God for that. Coz now I'm gonny enjoy ramming this pitchfork up your bliddy hell hole boy! Come here!

Nesbitt yanks Peter out of the doorway, and jabs him up the arse.

Peter yelps and races off down the street with Nesbitt in pursuit.

NESBITT. (*Pursuing.*) Get thee in front of me Satan!

A furniture van has pulled up in the street. Mary stands, watching Nesbitt chasing Peter.

MARY. (*Calling to Nesbitt.*) And when yiv finished that, Rab, maybe yi could gie the privet a trim, it's a disgrace! (*She snaps up a pair of old shears.*)

A sinister looking man carrying a large cooking pot appears before Mary, smiling. His name is Denis.

DENIS. (*His hand outstretched to Mary.*) Hi. I'm Denis. I'm just moving in next door.

MARY. Oh my God. And tell me, what's your social depravity?

DENIS. Och, I'm just a regular kind of guy. By day I work in a chocolate factory. And in my spare time I'm a serial killer. (*Indicates to the pot, shyly.*)

MARY. (*To audience.*) Well I suppose I better look on the bright side. At least they keep themselves to themselves.

Denis picks up a hat box, smiles at Mary. Mary smiles back.

MARY. (*To audience.*) Bliddy neighbours!